Zora Prosperi at age 8 (1919)

Acknowledgments

Thanks to my husband, Richard, who labored
lovingly over the manuscript and who read
version after version.
To my cousin, Peter Lucchesi, I send grateful
sentiments for his own memories and profound
understanding of family lore.
My brother, Bill, and my daughter, Daria, were
generous with their enthusiasm and support
to this fledgling author.
I would also like to thank my writing coach,
Kelly Ferjutz, for her invaluable editing,
encouragement and experience.

ZORA

The Life of an Ordinary Girl

Living in

Extraordinary Times

by

Gloria Hanson

2009

ZORA
The Life of an Ordinary Girl Living in
Extraordinary Times

by:

Copyright © 2009 Gloria (Lucchesi) Hanson

ISBN: 1449926215

EAN-13: 9781449926212

Chapter 1
A Girl and Marriage

W ho was this handsome stranger who appeared in the Riolo church square on a cloudy day in November of 1928? He was dressed in a suit, sporting a tie and a fine gentleman's hat that was obviously not Italian. He cut quite a figure and caught the eye of the young girls coming to fill their water bottles or *fiaschi* at the village fountain. He wore leather shoes and carried a valise of the same material, standing in sharp contrast to the farmers in their dreary grey baggy pants and jackets.

The older kerchiefed women stared out the windows of their stone houses and tried to identify the young man who seemed to know his way around the cobbled streets as he ambled to a house in the Balso, the lower part of town. As he walked, he would tip his hat to the *signoras*, revealing a head of wavy brown hair, Roman profile and a compelling voice as he called them by name.

Some scratched their heads in wonder. Ever since the great migration beginning in the late 1800's, many villagers, both young and old, had left to seek a better life. Who could blame them? Life in small mountain villages was a grueling one as the men and women planted vegetables and fruit trees on the landscaped

1

mountain steppes or fields, shot birds to eat, and raised chickens, goats, rabbits and pigs to survive the long winters. The chestnut trees, planted by the Romans as they traveled north, provided the basic daily sustenance of flour to make pancake-like *necci*, and the grape vines gave some opportunities to make table wine in the good years.

Days began with outings to get wood for the fire, water for the coffee and eggs from the chickens while afternoons were filled with communal bread baking, hunting for birds, tending the fields or steeping the clothes in large vase-shaped vessels with burlap and ashes, followed by a three day soaking over the kitchen fire. The clothing and linens would then be rinsed in the backyard pool or *pozzo*, a rectangular stone structure with a scrubbing stone on one end, in ice-cold water and lugged to the lines to dry. Dinner meant more labor to cook over the flames in the fireplace, wash the dishes and scrub the pots and pans.

Spent, the women would knit and talk by the fire while the men would play cards by candlelight in the local taverna or *dopo lavoro*. Bedtime was early and swift since undressing meant a cold cutting-to-the bone in winter and only the heated ceramic tiles placed in the beds by loving wives and mothers saved many delicate souls. Nighttime trips to the outhouse involved more cold, more discomfort and even more misery.

Fathers and adolescent sons left their families for the Promised Land where they could find jobs and make money, thereby abandoning the life of scratching for survival. Prosperity had never come to the mountain towns so between 1876 and 1926 more than sixteen million Italians left for the New World or other parts of Europe.

"Ah, I know him," bellowed the white haired Vittoria as she peeked out her window, "He is Marianna's son, the runt of the Lucchesi litter. All her children left home following the old man who was moody and hard; and poor Marianna was left behind to fend for herself in the house her husband had built with his large mason's hands. I had never seen such large hands on a man. Maybe her son has come to take her with him."

Vittoria was the dominating figure in the Prosperi family, towering over her husband, a man with wavy hair swept to the side of his small head and sporting a curled mustache; he who catered to her every whim when he was in town. He, too, traveled to America to make money, but he wanted to return home and buy land with his riches and become a wealthy squire with acres of forests to be cut and chestnut trees to offer the sustaining milled flour favored by most Italian peasants.

Their sons, Paolo, Emo and Alfeo had left for the new world, as had their oldest daughter, Melba, who had married one of the Lucchesi clan, Arimede. The only remaining child was the young Zora who was anointed to train as a seamstress and stay with Mom. Vittoria was in no mood to lose another child to America. She had no desire to live alone and maintain the household. Yes, she enjoyed the perks of the wandering mate who provided well, making them one of the better off families in the village, but she wanted to live here in relative comfort with a daughter to help her and save her from loneliness.

Zora was no beauty, but she was attractive and intelligent yet unwilling to buck her powerful mother.

3

She dressed well in her ankle length shift dress showing off her shapely legs and narrow feet in leather heels. The long strand of beads led the eye to her round face and blue eyes that sparkled with curiosity and to her brown hair drifting to her waist and fastened away from her cheeks with a silver brooch. She had attended grade school and was planning to leave the village to attend school in the bustling town of Bagni di Lucca, a one half hour walk from Riolo in the Tuscan Appenine mountains.

Meanwhile, Marianna, the thin, small-waisted mother who had borne a brood of children at a young age, wore a dour look on her delicate face that was caressed by a strong, determined jaw. She was the youngest child in the Benvenuti family of eight, had married a tall, lanky Lucchesi named Pietro who was a stonemason by trade and the oldest in his family of eight. The couple had always struggled with their own family of six children, one of whom had died of leukemia in his second year. Being the breadwinner of one of the poorest families in the village, Pietro was forced to travel to America.

At the age of 30 he set off from Le Havre in France and worked in the States for a few years until he set forth again to return home. He had been a morose man who had suffered periods of extreme irritability and angry outbursts against his wife and children as his large workman's hands had landed on all of them. In 1904 he disappeared. No one knew what had become of him for months when he suddenly reappeared in Riolo.

He had been hospitalized in France for his depression, but the exact circumstances are still a mystery since families hid the shame of mental illness, a condi-

4

tion they did not understand. A few years later he developed diabetes and died in his forties from complications, leaving Marianna a widow dependent on her scattered children for financial support.

Now she looked upon her young son who appeared prosperous and happy. Why had he come back to Riolo? She could only speculate. She knew that he was doing well in America being a construction worker and salesman. What was his motive? Visit her? Show his success? Find a bride? Wait and see. Patience. It would all be made clear in time. There is only wasted time to fill with worries. Furthermore, she would never think of asking such a question. As a woman, mother and northern Italian, one did not inquire about such things; linens—whether dirty or clean—were not to be washed in public, neither did one hope for revelation from a family member. She would bite her tongue and hope—hope that he had come to take her to live with him in America where she could be near her children. She was tired of being alone.

The newly arrived visitor, Guglielmo Peter (*Pietro*) Lucchesi, known as Bill or Willy in the United States but Gulie here in Italy, was a twenty two-year-old bachelor who had left home at fifteen to find his fortune since there was no future for him in his mountain village. He had attended school for four years and had no interest in squeezing out a meager living in Italy or being conscripted into the Italian army. He would follow his brothers and sail to America where he could work and build a life.

Following a perilous journey in steerage of the *Dante Alighieri* he had arrived at Ellis Island on August 3, 1921. He had met his brother, Arimede, and traveled

with him and other Italian *"paisani"* or fellow countrymen, selling plaster of Paris statues of Jesus, the Blessed
Virgin Mary or piggy banks to American or Italian
housewives in the Philadelphia area. He tired of all that
walking from door to door in hot weather with only a
pittance to show for all his labor so he decided to travel
to Portland, Oregon and Seattle, Washington to work in
construction.

"Go West, young man, go west" he was told so he
hopped a train in September and traveled six days and
nights to reach the Pacific Ocean. Construction work on
the roads and the rail lines was grueling, and despite
the strength in his large hands, he was slight of build
and delicate in constitution, struggling to keep up with
the pace of the work line. The food cooked by his
roommates did not agree with him, and he missed his
mother's pasta and hearty soups.

"Ah, for a few slices of prosciutto and crusty Italian
bread, a bowl of pasta or even a plate of *necci* and sausage." he lamented.

Spending a year as a construction worker convinced
him to return to the northeast where his sister Dina had
married and settled in a small Connecticut town of Putnam. After immigrating in 1918, she had worked in a
foundry and then a woolen mill, married and had managed with her husband, Primo, to save enough money
to buy a small grocery store. Gulie settled nearby and
found work on the Putnam-Danielson rail line but later
traveled with his brothers selling statues in Schenecta-
dy, Detroit, Chicago, Syracuse and Milwaukee. He had
seen much of America and had become more successful
and happy as a salesman and businessman than a la-
borer. He saved his earnings despite his fondness for

fine clothing, shoes and pretty women whom he wooed despite his fractured English, relying on his seductive blue eyes and easygoing personality to make him a compelling character to the ladies.

Now he strolled around the village and reconnected with the locals who remembered him either as a young adolescent with a glib tongue or a good person to hunt with since he was a crack shot who usually bagged his prey. During the day he would help his mother with the chores around the house while at night he would play cards with the village men in the dimly lit *botega* up the street from his home.

One evening he happened to look up at the Prosperi house and notice that someone was peaking from behind the shutters. With his usual bravado he gave a wink and hoped it was not the woman of the household who had no use for people living in the lower end of town. The figure quickly popped back into the shadows, but this little game of hide and go seek would continue each evening. He had seen most of the young women in the town and had considered speaking to one or two, but this mysterious little window creature had piqued his curiosity.

He summoned up his courage and approached the door of the stone house one Sunday afternoon following mass at the Church of St. Nicholas across the piazza from the Prosperi house. He had donned his Sunday best and looked quite dapper as he knocked on the wooden door and waited for a response. A few minutes later, a tall, white-haired, imposing Vittoria Prosperi opened the door and stared with steely blue eyes at the young visitor.

"Good morning, Signora Prosperi. I am Gulie, son

of Marianna and Pietro. I have come to say hello and bring news of your family in America."

"I know who you are. You can come in now, but we are busy cooking so you cannot stay long," she answered briskly, forgetting the village tradition of hospitality and welcome.

She stepped away from the door and allowed him to enter. She wore a loose black dress covered by a bibbed apron in starched white muslin; a print kerchief wrapped her head and tied at the back of the neck in the old fashioned style. She invited him to sit down at the long kitchen table in front of the fireplace where a heavy iron pot was heating over a crackling fire. Long strands of pasta were basking in flour on the table and someone was standing by the sink cleaning pots and pans with large buckets of water sitting patiently by. He noticed that the scrubber was a young woman with brown hair and a womanly figure, dressed in a brown dress hanging to her slender ankles and showing only a glimpse of stockinged legs that sat in brown leather shoes. She had not turned to greet him, but after he had been seated and begun talking about the family members in America, she turned and nodded, sitting as a demure, respectful child in awe of her imposing mother.

There certainly was a spark there, and he tried to be introduced to the shy young girl, but Vittoria would have none of this. She sat stone-faced as he rambled on about the New World and the Prosperi family abroad. This monologue would have been cut short with the visitor being sent on his way, but the welcomed appearance of Alessio, the man of the house, who had returned from the city offices in Bagni di Lucca where he registered his land purchases saved the visitor from dismissal. Alessio was a friendly gentleman who had crossed the Atlantic many times to work and earn money so he could return home and invest in real estate. He greeted Gulie whom he had met in Connecticut, and he finally asked his wife to make coffee for the guest. Vittoria did not respond but nudged her daughter who immediately rose to grind the coffee beans and heat the water. She served the strong coffee in small glass cups and then proceeded to return to the perch by her mother. Alessio finally introduced his daughter to the visitor and spoke of her industrious and intelligent nature. Vittoria frowned and gave her husband "the look" to stop his prattling. Was her husband trying to arrange a match? No way would she lose another child to the New World and to a poor workingman with an uncertain future. She had plans for this daughter and intended to speak to Alessio about his matchmaking speeches.

Gulie thought that it was time to leave since he could sense a tension in the room. He thanked his hosts for the hospitality, nodded to Vittoria and the girl, Zora, and quietly made his exit. He would have to inquire about this young woman who appealed to him and also think about how he would charm the mother who was intent on shielding her daughter from all suitors. This was not going to be as easy as the other girls he had wooed whose families had welcomed him with open arms. Perhaps he could find Zora alone when she was looking for firewood or getting water at the fountain. Then he could strike up a conversation to determine whether she was interested in getting to know him thus getting her out from under the yoke of her overprotective and possessive mother. This would be a challenge, but he had never avoided risk, especially in matters of the heart.

Back at the Prosperi household, Alessio was getting an earful from his wife. He listened and nodded but had no intention of compliance, thinking that if his daughter could join the others in America then Vittoria would have to agree to try the New World. He knew that none of the children would return to live in Riolo, and he was tired of going back and forth from the Old to the New World as he was losing hope of becoming a rich man in Italy; he decided that he would quietly encourage the match between the Prosperi and Lucchesi clan. He would send Zora on errands where she might meet up with Gulie. He knew that, if interested, the Americano would take care of the rest.

And so these rendezvous would occur under Vittoria's nose. The young people were obviously interested in one another and became unconsciously complicit in the plot. They thought they were getting away with something by meeting and talking in the town square, the pasture where the chestnut trees bloomed, or the path to the next village. Soon they would walk hand in hand and sometimes stop to embrace.

They decided that they would make a good team; and if they could persuade her parents to consent, they would move to America and build a life there. Gulie had made the New World seem like a land of milk and honey, streets made of gold and Zora, the young innocent, became caught up in the excitement of the future, being in love she did not bother to ask questions about the actual living conditions and the many challenges ahead. She would soon discover reality.

Following the Christmas holidays, Gulie and Zora

decided to approach her parents. Vittoria felt blindsided and angry that her usually obedient daughter had disobeyed her and had been meeting with this rogue. She was certain that all he wanted was a workhorse to help him become established and successful and since Zora was an easygoing, passive girl who wanted to please those around her she would become "an indentured servant" and lose any chance to gain a solid profession and even a small semblance of independence. If she attended school in Bagni di Lucca, she would be able to have a larger pool of bachelors from which to choose and could perhaps marry well. Being close to home, she would be the one left behind to care for her aging parents.

"These are the shattered dreams of a mother and the frustrations of a wife," she thought to herself. Perhaps she and Alessio could dissuade their daughter or at least delay the liaison until she was older.

Disappointment again—Alessio offered his wife no assistance. He seemed delighted and coolly, as head of the family, gave his consent to the marriage. Speechless, Vittoria sat in frozen anger and disgust as the young couple described their plans to wed in February, honeymoon in Venice and then leave for America from the port of Genoa. They would marry in the local church with not much fanfare since the date was imminent.

Vittoria didn't sleep much that night. She was too busy trying to understand how this had happened without her knowing. No one in the town had gossiped to let her know what was going on so they must have had a partner in their deceit.

"Ahhh! She cried, "It must have been my own husband." Who else? She would never forgive him. Indeed, despite her decision to try the New World several years later, she abruptly stated to him that she wanted to return home. She did not like America, would never live there, and wanted her village life back—with or without a husband or a child to care for her.

Chapter 2
The Voyage

*T*he ship was the same one that had brought Zora's father home many times. It was not a luxury ship, and Gulie could only afford second-class tickets, but it was certainly better than the one he had sailed on as a young man of fifteen. The *Dante Alighieri* had been in service for many years, but when in steerage for $25, the traveler did not have a room or even a shared room. The immigrants traveled in a cramped, unhealthful below-deck space where foul air, seasickness residues, bad food and disease reigned for the 8 to 20 day passage.

Upon arrival the survivors had to obtain a *nulla osta*, a certification stating that there were no legal impediments to their arrival. The shipping companies, fearing that they would be fined for carrying immigrants who did not pass the test, required passengers to take disinfectant baths, fumigate their luggage and submit to a medical examination. Having reached Ellis Island they would step from the ship onto a wooden ramp leading to the main building where doctors would survey their bodies looking for signs of tuberculosis, measles, hair and nail fungus or trachoma.

If one passed that ordeal, the weary traveler would wait in a room with thirty others to be interrogated by officials with the help of interpreters. With even a slight delay, the immigrant waited more hours, often days until authorization and proper documents were secured.

Gulie remembered that first time and cringed at the vivid memory. He told the full story to Zora who felt relieved that she would not have had to endure that ignominy since she was a citizen through her own father's citizenship. Now her new husband had insured her safe passage with a ticket. She comforted her new husband telling him that she hoped he would never have to go through that ordeal again and that she would always be there to care for him.

"What is it going to be like in America?" Will we have to live with strangers? Will we have running water? A toilet? Our own room?" she asked.

"I can only tell you that it will become easier as we work hard, save our money and start something for ourselves. At first, it will be difficult; but yes, we will have running water in our apartment, a bathroom nearby and inside the house, not outside in the yard or on the veranda. Americans use coal to heat their houses; we won't have to go and collect wood in the forest and carry it on our heads. "

"Who will come to meet us in New York? How do we get around from place to place? We walked everywhere in Italy, but I understand that America is a big country and difficult."

"My brother, Arimede, will meet us and take us by automobile to a place called Connecticut where there are other family members working in the factories. My sister, Dina, is there and will help us with a place to live until we have enough money to get our own apartment."

"I am relieved since I have never been away from home and my mother. I wake up with nightmares about what is going to happen to us. Ever since that Mussolini came into power in our country, I have been afraid of the future."

The Italian people had been caught in the middle of the conflict between the socialists and the fascists. After WWI the nationalists and the left wing socialists battled each other, and because the Italians had not been ceded the Dalmatian coast in the Treaty at Versailles, the once socialist Mussolini revived the "fasces" emblem of the old Romans and founded a new party in 1919—the Fascists. They planned to seize financial capital, develop councils, confiscate church lands and abolish the monarchy and the Senate.

Mussolini fused the old nationalistic myths of militarism and domination together with a Futuristic myth of Italy as a socialistic entity. Initially not a violent man, Mussolini turned to physical terror after the Socialists split into communists and socialists who spilled blood when they attempted to take over the State. Mussolini responded by forming the "action squads" to deal with the chaotic elements in society and following his designation as "*Il Duce*" in 1921, he agreed to violence. Hence, 1922 became the year of terror, as the squads would go from city to city purging the local government of their radical members. The Fascists and Mussolini became unstoppable.

Italy was a poor country with high birth and inflation rates, and the War had divided, not united it. Parliament was corrupt, the monarchy was disrespected, and the state and Church were at odds. Chaos abounded since Italians were fearful of the Red Terror that fed tales of Lenin's atrocities. They couldn't stabilize public services. As a result Mussolini and his "Blackshirts" finally won approval to govern. For a few years, Mussolini governed with a desire to be loved and admired. He made the trains run on time and did not create a secret police or shut down the press, but after the murder of an opposition delegate, Giacomo Marreotti, at the hands of Il Duce's goons, Mussolini abandoned the socialists and liberals and became a dictatorial leader. The state became the head, body and soul. He described his brand of fascism as "an organized, concentrated, authoritarian democracy on a national basis" (Mussolini, *Opera Onmia*). Whoever had not left for the west during the Great Migration was fearful and made plans to flee their homeland for political and financial reasons. Most of the young people in the mountain villages had already made their decisions with their feet and had braved perilous journeys across the Atlantic to escape this *matto* or madman.

After seven days of rough waters, cloudy skies and seasickness, Guglielmo, known as Bill, and Zora, Americanized to Dora, landed on the lower east side of New York City where crowds of relatives, merchants, and immigrants milled around in seemingly chaotic fashion. Men in heavy boots, wooly sweaters and hats hawked everything from prosciutto to potatoes, from fish to slabs of beef, from old shoes to worn coats and gloves. Everyone was pushing and shoving to get to the wide-eyed and anxious passengers. How could anyone find a relative in that sea of faces and bodies? The smells alone would give a new immigrant pause and make her wonder if this venture had been a colossal mistake.

Bill helped his stunned and awed young bride

16

down to the wharf with small suitcase in hand. He peered over the crowd looking for a familiar face. The first time he had set foot on the new land he met his brother by the fish market down the street from the wharf. Arimede had been leaning against a barber's pole, had lit another cigarette and since he wasn't going to venture into the mass of humanity down by the dock, guessed his kid brother would find him sooner or later. Bill knew his brother and thought that this would be the same scenario since Arimede would go out of his way only so much for someone else. As Bill and Dora made their way through the crowd, they clutched each other's arms so as not be swept away in the wave of humanity. Dora wore a dazed, disturbed look but kept up the pace as the new husband shepherded her towards a new life. She thought that she must have been very brave—or very stupid—to hitch her wagon to a man she hardly knew.

The Voyage

Two love birds board.

"Sail us to Eden, where
gold-paved streets, and
money-growing trees await."

This is the fantasy.

See the lady holding
a torch, lighting the way?
Wide-eyed, open mouthed,
clutching the rail they
breathe a sigh of relief.

No naked savages come
to greet or eat them.
Seas of bearded faces
hawking their wares
crash against them.

Push, pull, crowd, move.
The wave carries two
innocent souls forward
toward the dream of today
into the reality of tomorrow.

gm hanson

Chapter 3
The New World and the New Life

*H*aving navigated the port of New York and the mass of humanity gathered there, Dora and Bill piled their trunk and suitcases into Arimede's old Ford and made their way out of the big city and onto the narrow roads leading to the state of Connecticut. The crowded streets of New York gave way to hills blanketed with tall oaks, chestnuts and a wide variety of lush vegetation. America certainly was green, and it reminded her of a flatter version of the Tuscan hill villages she had left behind.

Cars honked as they passed the slow moving Ford, but the noise did not seem to bother Arimede who smoked his cigarettes and kept his eyes on the road ahead. His driving skills were legend in the Lucchesi family. Anyone who had an alternate method of transportation took it, whether by donkey or horse-drawn carriage since his meandering style of driving put fears into the hearts of his brothers, sisters, wife and children, not to mention the other drivers on the road.

He was the first member of the clan Dora met, yet she felt she knew him from the stories of his escapades during his youth in Italy, of his roving eyes and his self-centered nature. He was the oldest child in a family of six born to Marianna of the Benvenutis and Pietro of the

Lucchesi clan and was also the frequent beneficiary of his father's heavy hand and dark moods.

Born in 1895, he quickly realized that the life of an Italian peasant would not suit his personality so he joined his father on a trip to the new land. His marriage to Dora's older sister, Melba, was greeted with the same disdain and disapproval by Vittoria. In a small mountain town, people know all the quirks of their neighbors' characters since the oral tradition of telling stories and gossiping about people led to strong opinions about the families themselves.

Nicknames were made up for families to characterize their core personalities. Many of these were pejorative; others claimed the fame of dead relatives. In the case of the Prosperi family, the nickname, "Grattini" referred to their supposed scratching for money. The Lucchesi clan was labeled the "Carlone" named after Carlo Lucchesi, the patriarch married to Alessandra who bore him an octet of offspring.

Arimede brought his wife to America and settled near his sister, Dina, in the New England town of Putnam, a curtain-manufacturing center. A few years ago his wife Melba had given birth to a girl and had named her Wanda. Melba was a dour woman, resembling her mother Vittoria and had the same ambitious, pretentious nature. Arimede, having worked selling statues and in construction work, had amassed enough money to buy a small grocery store with another Italian from their village.

As new family members crossed the ocean and settled near their families, they would work in Arimede and Melba's store. It was a difficult business since the hours were long and the work physically demanding.

New employees were eager to move on, as was Arimede who was talented at being the boss but not so good at physical labor, long hours and fussy customers. Dora was to find out more than she imagined about this business and this interesting man soon enough.

Arriving at the home of Dina and Primo Lucchesi, Dora was greeted warmly by her new sister-in-law. Dina was the second child in the Lucchesi family and had come to America in 1918 working in the factories around the town of Webster, Massachusetts where she, as an energetic and feisty woman, believed in and fought for unions. She gave birth to her first child, Norma, in 1920 shortly after purchasing a grocery store on the upper east side of Putnam and returned to work since she had hired an Italian neighbor to care for her child. It was common in those difficult days for both parents to work and leave childcare to family or neighbors.

She used her strong peasant sturdiness, quick mind and intelligence together with her genteel, accommodating husband Primo, always by her side doing the heavy lifting, to build their business. She was available to members of her family who would seek her advice and opinion because they viewed her as an immigrant success story.

Her husband was a gentle, easygoing man who worked hard to choose the best produce at the fruit and vegetable markets in Massachusetts and Rhode Island while helping his wife in the kitchen, as he loved to cook while chewing his Stogie cigar. They lived in an apartment house situated along the Quinebaug River where mills had been erected in the late 1860's and 1870's to manufacture cotton and woolen goods.

The area of northeastern Connecticut had become known for its textile factories, and French-Canadian, English and Irish immigrants poured into the area looking for work if you didn't have enough money to be an entrepreneur and open a business. There was always work in the flourishing mills of this part of New England. The Italians moving into the area preferred the life of salesman or shopkeeper as the path to prosperity. They had brought their independent, entrepreneurial spirit with them.

The rooms in Dina's apartment were large, comfortable, clean and heated—something that shocked and surprised Dora who had been accustomed to the minimal fireplace heat that might make its way to the rooms upstairs. Furniture was large and bulky, leftover from the Victorian era, but it was kept polished and protected with the lacy embroidered pieces brought over from the old country. The floors were covered with linoleum of various colors in the kitchen while darkly stained wooden floors graced the other rooms.

There were overhead lights in every room, and soft, billowy curtains with valances covered every window. A little room down the hall revealed a toilet with water, a box above with a long chain to flush it, a sink with two spigots and a white bathtub on clawed feet. Dora was awestruck. Were her eyes deceiving her—a bathtub in the house? Her family had a large metal tub to be filled with hot water that was heated over a fire. After each family member had her turn, she would have to drain it by the pailful.

What a treat it had been to go down the mountain to the baths in Bagni di Lucca where hot water and steam were available without backbreaking labor. Sitting on those marble benches had been a heavenly experience. She had heard that famous English poets called Percy Bysshe Shelley and John Keats had visited there to "take the healthy waters" and enjoy the steam rooms and warmth while traveling to Rome. Hopefully she would enjoy a tub in her own apartment as Bill had promised.

The two women began to gather the food Dina and Primo had prepared for their guests.

"So how do you like being married after leaving your parents and traveling across the world?" asked Dina as she efficiently set the table and tended to the cooking.

"Well, I think it's a grand adventure so far, but I must admit that I find it overwhelming and scary at times. I am happy to have a husband to take care of me because I can't imagine doing this alone as my husband did."

"We do what we have to do and hope for the best," the philosophical Dina responded, "I had no choice, and no husband who was more familiar with this country than I was so I knew that I would manage on my own. You will learn that soon enough because this is not an easy society and Bill won't always be around to watch over you and pave the way despite his having been here for some time."

"Yes, I guess I will have to grow up fast because I was the baby in my family and had no reason to want independence."

At the end of the meal there was a knock on the door and an immediate entrance of a tall, wavy-haired man who greeted his siblings and family warmly. He had not bothered to wait for an invitation to come in since this easy entry was the custom in the Italian villages and was transplanted to the new world. People expected family and neighbors to drop in at any time, at any hour.

Dora vaguely remembered this gentle giant who had married one of her distant cousins in the village of Riolo. Mini, the red-haired bride, and Elside had moved to America and settled near Putnam to begin a fruit and vegetable delivery service in the area. He was a private man, tending to be on the periphery of the family and keeping his own counsel.

He was the third child of the Lucchesi family and was to be the last. Instead Marianna gave birth to more children in the three years after his arrival. Sondra had arrived a year after his birth, William the year after that, and Philiberto in the following year. Elside was in the middle and received little attention from his parents or older siblings. As a result he found his own way. The death of his baby brother from childhood leukemia at fourteen months had devastated him since he was a sensitive soul who cared deeply. Marianna often said that the demise of her son had convinced her to put an end to her childbearing.

Dora and Bill set up their household a few weeks later as they found an apartment on Main Street in Danielson, another curtain town ten miles from Putnam. The flat was small with a kitchen, bath, living room and bedroom where one could see Danielson Fruit Company, the grocery of Arimede and Melba.

Dora was going to work there while Bill accompanied his father-in-law, Alessio, his brother-in-law Alfeo and a few other *paisani* or countrymen to Detroit where they would be making statues of religious figures, Botticelli angels to dispel the evil spirits that could destroy them, fruits and vegetables in bright colors resembling the perfect hues found in the sunny, southern Italian countryside.

"We have to be flexible," Bill said to Dora. "These separations will be frequent until we earn enough money to buy a store for ourselves, but now we have to sacrifice for the future."

"Why can't I go, too? I could cook and help you paint the statues. I don't want to live alone here where I don't know the language and have to depend on your family and my sister."

"Life on the road is not for a woman, Dora. We men live together in a small flat near the plant, eat pasta and salami day after day, and work from dawn to dusk in a dusty, dirty place. If all goes well, I will return in a few months with enough money to show my family that I am serious and could run a business with a little help from them. I suspect that Arimede wants to sell the Danielson store and open one in Putnam so this would be a golden opportunity for us to take over this grocery. Keep working, learning about this business and saving the money you earn so we can have a better life some day."

"This is your dream, and I support it, but I feel alone and out of place. Can't I at least go to school to learn the language? Then, I could move to the front of the store and sell instead of being a backroom mule." Dora had immediately sized up the situation at Danielson Fruit, and it did not look appealing.

"Going to school will have to wait. You have enough schooling to do numbers and write. Listening to the customers will help you understand a little of what they are requesting. We will pick up the language we need in the store and speak Italian at home so we won't forget our homeland."

That was that. Dora had no choice but to give in to her husband. Her father had told her that the husband was the "*capo*" or the head of the family and knew better. Patience and faith in the wisdom of the family kept her compliant and crossing the street each morning to her first job at Danielson Fruit.

The business was on the Main Street, nestled between the butcher's shop run by the Savage family and the automobile parts store owned by the Wards. There it was in all its glory, the melting pot on Main Street displaying the origins and religions of the people: white Anglo-Saxon Protestants, Roman Catholics and Jews from countries in Europe and Canada. These were the small business people, the backbone of this town.

The residents included immigrants from Finland and Greece, and if one looked hard enough one could find a few "Negroes" from the south living "on the other side of the tracks." The owners of the mills and lumber businesses were the "old families" who descended from the original Northern European immigrant migration. Hidden in the woods of the area were the Pequot-Mashintauk, Nipmuc and Mohegans, American Indian tribal people who had been displaced and lived a meager existence away from the invader communities.

This was not the chaotic, fast-paced and sophisticated area of New York or Chicago where gangland crime and jazz age music dominated and where buying on credit or installments was the order of the day. In those areas of the United States of America there were skyscrapers, baseball mania, Broadway musicals and the literary disillusionment and alienation following World War I.

The young intellectuals had rebelled against the remaining vestiges of the Victorian era and introduced Freudian ideas into their writing, producing their own literary giants: Hemingway, James, Dreiser and Faulkner, to name a few. Harlem was undergoing a Renaissance of its own with its music and variety including the integrated jazz germinating there. Women would wear dresses with dropped waists, skirts to the knees, long tunics, gloves and shoes with buckles, bows and straps, and were looked upon as sexual symbols modeled on the child like cartoon character, Betty Boop, while the men who pursued women and success wore suits, ties and felt hats.

The nineteen twenties were the years of general prosperity for many, from the working and middle classes to the rich barons of industry. The government under Harding and even Coolidge believed that business was meant to pursue gain but also to apply a moral purpose and provide service to the society at large while regulating itself with minimal interference from government. There was a rise in national income—from $59.4 to $87.2 billion in eight years and individual family income going from $522 to $716 per year. Americans were spending and using credit, buying life insurance, homes, automobiles and a piece of industry called stocks.

The advances in the technology also propelled the economy as people bought radios and went to the movies. The improving financial climate spurred immigrants to Americanize, integrating into language and culture. Women could dress well, smoke and go to work or choose the "Blondie" life of homemaker, and children would be educated in free public schools. The bourgeois existence of personal identity and responsibility moved people away from the collective experience of village life. The prosperity was spotty; and President Coolidge, a fiscal conservative, feared economic trouble and refused to run in 1928.

In the mill towns and farms where people struggled to survive and put food on the table, life was slower and harder. Families would gather around the radio and hear about the good life in the big cities, lose themselves in the radio soap operas and drama shows, but they had little time to play Mah Jong or dance in the marathons. Women, having won the right to vote in 1920, were still separated according to socioeconomic class.

The immigrant influx had slowed since the government, influenced by high racial and ethnic tensions and the Red Scare, established quotas favoring peoples from northern Europe. The music the village folk enjoyed was that of the sentimental ballads, Grand Ole Opry and Al Jolson. Yes, the country was shrinking because of the automobile, radio and movies, but the demands of daily life curtailed any devotion to entertainment and frivolity in small town America.

On October 29, 1929, Black Tuesday, the city came to the countryside as the stock market crashed and banks closed their doors. Payrolls began to drop and millions would lose their jobs in the thirties. The Great Depression had eclipsed the prosperity of the early twentieth century.

The enormous affluence of the twenties had only trickled down to the farmers and textile workers and their bosses, but the long-term effects of this economic crisis were felt in the inability to get credit, the fall in farm prices and the distrust people developed in financial institutions. Many ordinary Americans had begun to put their savings into the stock market and homes, but this slowed in the thirties as life in the Northeastern mill towns became more difficult as the Depression spread throughout the country and the world. Bread lines and ruined businesses were common occurrences.

Dora had never experienced food deprivation since the food in her Italian home might have been monotonous and basic, especially in the winter; but there was always enough. The good thing for Dora and her relatives in America was that neighbors and fellow citizens did need to eat.

Zora at 16

Alessio & Vittoria 1901

Vittoria & Dora 1921

Vittoria and children   1914

Paolo, Melba, Vittoria, Zora, Emo, Alfeo

30

(rear)   Marianna, Elside
(front) Pietro, Dena, Guglielmo

Dina and Elside

Marianna

Dora and Bill 1929

Cut off my ear, Wall Street

Glory days are gone,
listing in the wind, the ship
opens for state business,
running from the Bears
in reaction to bad news.
Again we bail out greed,
saps, suckers, sycophants.

Lavish, shameless life styles,
all at taxpayers' expense
moving golden money around
encircling the gaslit globe.
Not to worry or fret!
Tell us you still trust us.
Send out the soothsayers.

Move on, Oh Ship of State.

gm hanson

Chapter 4
Business – American style

*D*anielson Fruit was the typical blueprint store for small town businesses. Two large display windows bordered a long glass door encased in wood that was set back to provide a short walkway. A striped awning was rolled down on summer mornings to protect the outdoor stands filled with mounds of fruit looking freshly picked and ready to eat—peaches, pears, cherries, cantaloupes, berries and bananas. Sitting on guard in the lower rows lay the rotund watermelons awaiting the eye of the strolling Main Street pedestrian. In the evening those that had not been taken to new homes were brought inside for safekeeping, and the awning was carefully rolled up for the night.

Inside, the long corridor of the wooden floor led to a back preparation room. As one entered the front door, one's senses were treated to the fragrance of fruits and vegetables neatly placed in slanting shelves along the left side while canned goods from the likes of the prestigious SS Pierce brands colorfully lit up the right wall. The shelves were tall-from floor to ceiling, and Dora would use a pincer like tool and hope that it would not fall on her head.

"Maladetto te" or "damn you," she would mutter under her breath since she didn't want to lose a customer because of foul language or her clumsiness.

A tall brass cash register stood in a nook along the wall on one side of the far end of the store, and a small three-foot radiator nestled on the other side. Breads from Wonder Bakery and Fleishman's nestled near the Devil Dogs and Twinkies. Paper goods and tobacco completed the inventory as cigarettes were stored by brands in the slots of a wooden wall holder while cigars lay in their wooden beds nearby.

Chesterfields, Pall Malls and Camels invited men to buy a pack or two while stogies and expensive cigars lured the brave masculine souls who would light up anywhere and everywhere. Dora would complain of the smell and the smoke since Bill would always have a cigarette dangling from his mouth or take along a cigar when driving or relaxing.

A large walk-in refrigerator held pride of place in the preparation room at the back of the store, along with a sink that had running cold water for rinsing the mounds of produce stored in the wooden boxes piled high against the wall. There was also a table for constructing fruit baskets or wrapping vegetables plus storage shelves packed with brown wrapping paper, yellow, red, green or orange cellophane to encircle the gift boxes. Rolls of string, ribbon and bows unraveled from their spindles with a flick of the wrist.

The back door opened to a large parking lot near the railroad tracks where long train cars would pass by every morning and afternoon with a conductor who would wave and blow the whistle to clear the tracks of kids wanting to flatten their pennies on the tracks.

Dora was impressed with the layout, and she marveled at all the items on the shelves, the fresh fruits and vegetables and the sheer variety of it all.

"America certainly is the land of plenty" she mused. "I think I will like working here even though it does seem to be a little cold inside."

"You'll get used to it," Bill assured her as he wrapped her in a long white apron and set her to wash the spinach that had just arrived from the market in Providence.

"What? Wash all that spinach? I hate spinach."

There seemed to be a mound of never-ending, never-diminishing spinach needing to be rinsed in the cold water gushing from the spigot. Her delicate hands recoiled from the chill, but she was determined to be a good worker and an obedient wife. At night she would try to shake off the icy cold she felt in her hands and feet by snuggling close to Bill as she dreamed of spinach mountains and gushing waterfalls.

"Do Americans really like spinach?"

"I'm afraid so, my dear, I'm afraid so, because they believe it gives them strength and stamina, as Popeye says," Bill claimed, trying to re-assure his doubting, trembling spouse.

Dora's inability to speak English would keep her out of the sales area except for packing the shelves, sweeping the floor or carrying bags to the customers' cars parked in front of the store. In this somewhat isolated position, she was at a disadvantage for learning the native language. Would she ever be able to go to school to learn this complicated language where most words sounded so guttural and unnatural compared to her mellifluous Italian? What would her mother say about this state of affairs when she visited next year? Vittoria would see her daughter in the backroom washing vegetables in cold water, packing, unpacking, lifting boxes of fruits and tending to the fire in the basement where the furnace required constant feeding of wood and coal.

"You are nothing but a workhorse, my dear daughter. You should have listened to your mother and stayed in Italy. By now you would have been a graduate of grade school and trained as a seamstress working in a warm shop and perhaps married to the shop owner. Look at you now."

Dora and Bill 1934

The Job

Is there anyone who doesn't love a job?
To organize one's life, to give meaning
In this vale of tears, this chaotic universe
Avenging those nighttime demons of failure?

He brings home a paycheck for his troubles
And drops a few crumbs of himself
At the feet of his loyal, soft spoken spouse
Who used to complain of leftovers, now sighs.

What drives these men to seek and strive?
Is success a beguiling wench who
Sits on the rock promising eternity?
Or a siren who sings of fame and fortune?

He walks with struggle to leave a footprint
On this shifting sands of earth
Kicking the little pebbles to the side
Giving little notice to their cries for attention

Who will remember his toil in a few?
The hard work will be forgotten
But the memories of the child set aside
Will forever haunt the old gray head.

gm hanson

Chapter 5
Hard Times

*T*he early thirties were difficult ones for most Americans as the Great Depression left its mark despite the initial attempts of President Hoover and the bold attempts by Franklin Roosevelt to intervene and shore up the economy. The unemployment rate was still around 14.3% in 1937 despite the billions spent on new roads, buildings, bridges, airports, sewer systems, parks and recreational facilities. The rolls of the unemployed had reached as high as 25%. The American economy sputtered until 1939 when the news of the war in Europe stimulated growth in preparations for war. Until that time Americans had lost faith in the free market economy, and intellectuals looked eastward towards the socialist state like Russia for inspiration.

During the years of struggle from 1929 to 1939 Bill and Dora had become flexible travelers, going from job to job trying to stay afloat. Dora's mother, Vittoria, had come and gone. She traveled to the United States at the urging of her husband and children, but after a seven month trial she said, "*Basta, voglio retorna a casa mia,*" "Enough, I want to return to my home."

And that is exactly what she did. She never returned to her family in America. Despite wars and turbulence she would not leave her country or her mountain village. "If they want to see their mother, they can travel here," she would announce to friends and relatives who questioned her decision. Dora would remember those words when she tussled with her conscience as the years passed and no visiting was possible.

Bill, accompanied occasionally by Dora, would live and work selling statues in Connecticut towns, in Providence, Rhode Island, Brooklyn, New York and Chicago, Illinois as they searched for new markets for their wares. Times were tough since extra money was hard to come by for most Americans, but Italian-Americans and other Catholics could not resist a statue of Jesus with open arms and Mary, the bountiful mother. Their faith and Plaster of Paris reminders would allow them to find a few dollars for a symbol of hope in the future.

Then, quite unexpectedly, Arimede and Melba decided to travel to the homeland and left Bill and Dora in charge of their business, allowing Bill to settle in one place and join his wife and family. They had saved for so long, hiding their money in stockings and underwear or wearing it on their bodies while they peddled statues. Bill and Dora approached their siblings as soon as they returned home from Italy with an offer to purchase Danielson Fruit thereby giving Arimede the freedom to open a new establishment in nearby Putnam where he had purchased a multifamily home on a hill above town.

The deal was sealed, and Dora and Bill were ecstatic. It had taken them four years to become independent owners.The dark nightmares of perpetual poverty and seeing themselves as the "black sheep" of the family were replaced with dreams filled with dancing stars and images of themselves as healthy, wealthy and wise.

"Now we can put down roots in this town and begin a real American life and live the American dream."

Bill declared as he piled the luscious golden-reddish Georgia peaches into a perfectly symmetrical pyramid.

"Yes, yes, and maybe we can start a family and buy a home." His wife responded with anticipation and delight, having seen the proud young mothers parade by with their perambulators carrying the chubby infants wrapped in pink or blue blankets. The call of motherhood was getting stronger.

"Whoa now, slow down, one thing at a time. We must first put all of our energies into building this business. We can't afford to go beyond that. Be patient. All will come in due time."

"I'm so tired of practicing patience, but I guess I have no choice."

The hours were long, the work demanding and tedious as they had so many things to remember, so many records to keep, so much cleaning, sweeping and straightening. They had made a commitment to order and cleanliness, quality and service, and now they had to deliver. Bill decided that he would put his trust in the bank where he would make his weekly deposits.

This decision was difficult since banks had been failing during the Great Depression; but his even greater hesitancy was based on the Italian distrust of institutions, especially institutions of finance. The tendency to be an Italian anarchist was bred into the bones, anxiety and paranoia imprinted in the brain; but now that he was an American businessman, he must learn to think American. And so he did, putting his trust in a local bank.

The close affiliation with the other families in the grocery business helped sustain Danielson Fruit. Bill would share the trips to the Providence market, a sprawling area by the railroads, with his brother Arimede and brother-in-law Primo. The driver would have to arise at 3AM and travel the roads to pick up the fruits and vegetables, drop these items off to the other stores and arrive at his own business in time to display the fresh produce by 9AM.

It was a grueling exercise for these young men, and the haggling for the best fruits and vegetables at the lowest price together with the loading of the boxes onto their trucks added to the anxiety and strain. The cigarette and the cigar would make it bearable for them, and a stop at the roadside tavern for a beer lessened the load.

The immigrant experience made for cooperation and conflict in families who were dependent on each other to survive in these hard times. This is not to say that the load was borne equally. Primo's family thought that he was doing more than others; yet Primo would not say much to his brother-in-laws since he wanted to be part of their fraternity, to be a band of brothers. For the most part they were united in the effort to succeed and were prepared to sacrifice for each other and their cause.

Socializing for these folks meant visiting each other's homes or apartments, sharing stories and a pasta meal. On those sweltering hot days of summer where the heat bent the air and only butterflies moved, the family would gather for a picnic at a forested state park where rocks, woods and water brought some relief. If one member fell on hard times, another was there to offer a helping hand with money or sweat labor. This was a strong familial community.

Children had been produced during the 1920's with the arrival of Norma for Dina and Primo and Wanda for Arimede and Melba. Girls were not highly valued in Italian families as they were looked upon as potential financial drains while boys were highly prized since they would carry the family name and inherit the business. Both Bill and Dora bought into these values. After seven years of marriage they decided to pursue parenthood. How they managed to remain childless for those years no one knew or bothered to ask.

There was widespread ignorance of birth control in early modern Christian Europe, especially since the population decline following the Black Death starting in 1348. The state began to influence and educate people to grow the population. Some scholars believe that witch-hunts were instituted as effective measures against the midwives; and governments as well as the male gynecologists hired to look after pregnant women, sanctioned these abuses or looked the other way.

For most of history birth control was under the control of women who used herbal remedies and taught barrier methods to help other women take charge of their bodies. Abortions were not unheard of, and wealthy women could have a "scraping" done to end an unwanted pregnancy. Abstinence, a late marriage, withdrawal or the unreliable condoms made of animal intestines were the most frequently used contraceptive methods. The Drafenberg ring, an intrauterine device, was introduced in 1928, but this method was available only to women of means.

In the USA of the nineteen twenties and thirties, a large family was seen as a threat to the socioeconomic well being of middle class Americans, but many saw the encroaching modern views as the real threat. The US outlawed abortions, and in 1936, they passed the Comstock Law making it illegal to send birth control through the US mail. Margaret Sanger (1879-1966) fought for the freedom of women to obtain birth control information in clinics she established between 1914-1937. The Comstock Law was declared unconstitutional, the war ended and the population exploded between 1946-1960 making the education of birth control methods easier for all Americans, should they be interested.

Dora continued to work during her pregnancy although she was told by her doctor to avoid lifting anything heavy. Yet her schedule continued to be dreary and demanding. She had no idea about childbirth since no one had bothered to instruct her. These issues were not discussed openly. Menstruation began—give her a pad. Married—hope for the best and rely on the husband to know what he was doing. Most women entered these major life events with blinders and endured. If Dora had been in Italy she would have had a midwife assist her at home, but here she would be taken to a hospital and put in a clean white-sheeted bed with nurses and doctors available to care for her.

In some ways, she thought, this will be a vacation from drudgery.

The doctor told Bill that he would have her in a "twilight sleep." This twilight anesthesia consisted of morphine to blunt the pain and scopolamine to induce amnesia. Hopefully she would not get an infection; and if she did, there was some new, untested medicine called an antibiotic that was under development, and might save her. She felt somewhat assured, but she still feared death in childbirth for either herself or the baby. Worried about her soul, Dora would vacillate between saying the rosary in the early contractions and praying to the Blessed Virgin Mother. She was alone in a room, afraid of the unknown and wishing her mother was nearby.

The baby finally made her appearance on April 16, 1936 at 10:30AM. Dora was a happy mother once she recovered from the twilight zone while Bill, hoping for a boy, passed out cigars and displayed a joyful spirit for family and for his wife. They decided to name the baby Gloria Marianna, the latter name in honor of Bill's mother.

Gloria was a brown-haired, blue-eyed tiny bundle who fussed and cried often and loudly. Once milk was delivered in the modern way—a bottle—she would fall into a deep sleep for a short while and then awaken to demand to be fed again. The transition to her new home and bassinet brought another display of pique. Marianna, who had come to stay in America, helped the young couple adjust to the new baby. She mused that this noisy beginning was just that—the beginning of a temperamental young life and the end of a full night's sleep for those taking care of this little bundle of joy.

The Virtues

Plato and the Church teach
us four cardinal virtues,

Forebear or endure.
Temper or restrain.
Seek justice and right
Practice prudence daily.

Saints and the Bible
urge the theological virtues.
Be steadfast in piety
hope in life and death.
Love selfishly and give.
Have you fallen prey to
vices betraying virtues?
Are you extravagant in
thought, word or deed?
Does gluttony rule your
mind, body and soul?
Do you give freely in
thought and action?
Have you pursued patience
or shown wrath and pride?

Does Freedom come to these followers?
Peace?
Joy?

gm hanson
May, 2009

Chapter 6
Three Full Time Jobs

W orking in the home, the store and the nursery was overwhelming for Dora who, although only twenty-three years old felt as if she were forty or fifty. Her mother-in-law, Marianna, lived with them; but this was a mixed blessing since the apartment was small and cramped, privacy a lost cause since the walls were thin, and the living quarters challenged anyone wanting to get a few moments alone. Dora began to eat more in order to keep the pace. She would snack on Devil Dogs and Coca Cola and eat hearty meals prepared by her mother in law and herself.

Marianna was the traveling *Nonna* or granny who moved from one of her children to the other when they started their families. She was the nanny who made the rounds; and having had the experience in the home, the nursery and the fields, she could cook, clean and care for children. Now she arose early in the morning to make breakfast, feed the baby, clean, make the beds, wash the cotton diapers by hand and hang them out on the clothes line to dry.

Then at noon she would make lunch for Bill who would return to the store and send Dora home for her meal. No sooner had Marianna cleaned up after lunch, she had to begin to prepare dinner and respond to the waking baby. At eight she would collapse onto the narrow bed in the nursery to prepare for the shift work of evening and early morning feedings and changing. She had thought that her days as a mother caring for babies were over after her sixth was born and that she could retire into a laid-back grandmotherly role. Yet it was better than sitting still in a big grey rocking chair waiting for people, ideas or death to arrive at your doorstep.

"I guess I should have stayed in Italy if I had wanted to be free from household drudgery and child care, but of course, I would then been a lonely, aging widow of Riolo, a small town in the middle of the warring nations of crazies."

The family appreciated her sacrifices and tried to take good care of her since they realized what a help she was to working parents. On summer Sunday afternoons, the families would get together at a local state park to eat and socialize. They could wade in the pond, enjoy the woodland paths and feel the warm sun on their skin. Marianna would sit in the shade in her dark ankle length dress, long black stockings and a kerchief holding back her graying hair.

Every family would bring a dish of pasta, meat or vegetables, and they would gladly carry the meal to Marianna who was free at last to sit and be waited upon as her station in life demanded. The women would congregate and talk about the old country, relatives and their long and weary days while the men sat by themselves smoking, drinking homemade wine and sharing their business stories.

This was an insular group who stayed by themselves because of language and cultural barriers. Italian was spoken because none of them were fluent in English and going to night school to learn the language meant time away from the store. It was difficult enough to attend church on Sundays, the supposed day of rest for most Americans but not for these ambitious Italians who kept the store open for their forgetful neighbors. So they learned as they went along, and it was not until the children went to school that they became more comfortable speaking English.

As Bill and Dora were the youngest members of the extended family, they received advice from everyone. The family decided that Bill and Dora's apartment was too small—a change was to be made. The relatives helped them move into a larger apartment near the Longo family who owned a spacious three-floor house near the Quinibaug River.

The widow, Catherine and her spinster daughters, Annie and Marion, lived on the first floor in an apartment that was a Victorian sampler. Doilies covered the overstuffed furniture, and a large piano filled much of the formal parlor. The Longos were so happy that an Italian family would occupy the second floor apartment, especially one with an Italian child. Marion would help as a salesperson in the grocery store. Everyone was happy. Dora and Bill were excited to have three bedrooms, a good-sized kitchen, dining room and parlor. Now the couple could breathe and enjoy a little privacy.

By then, Gloria was walking around and soon became the favorite of the landlady and her daughters. She could wander downstairs to bang on the piano and be spoiled by the women who loved her spirit and energy. Marianna did not complain since this would allow her a little relief.

Gloria was not a quiet, reserved child, and Marianna had to juggle many things to keep up with her. Everyone would try to feed this little girl, but she was not a normal Italian kid who would eat everything on her plate. Overfeeding was a common behavior in Italian immigrant families, and a rotund body something to be admired. The family tradition of eating well and stuffing little children could not be applied here. If they did succeed in getting her to eat, they would be awakened by the sound of the girl crying and vomiting her meal.

"Where did this child come from?" Aunt Melba would say. "She is so scrawny. Make her eat."

"I can't open her mouth and shove it in since she clamps her mouth shut and won't give in. I squeeze fresh orange juice in the morning, and when I am cooking her egg, she throws the drink into the toilet." Marianna complains.

Dora declares and defends, "She won't eat for anyone although sometimes she will nibble for Bill whom she adores, but she balks with him, too. We are worried about her, but the doctor says to be patient."

"She will eat when she is hungry. Give her an egg sweetened with sugar in a glass of milk and a teaspoon of cod liver oil. That way she will be getting nutrition."

Of course, the non-eating, skinny child did not fit into the family tradition where food was a centerpiece of life, a demonstration of their achievement in the New World and a reaction to the poverty of their origins. Every event was celebrated with food: pasta dishes made with plenty of Bolognese sauce, cheeses, salami, mortadella, prosciutto, roasts of beef, lamb or pork and greens slathered in olive oil. Hearty soups made with rich broth, beans and vegetables were winter staples as was the homemade wine.

Each summer, the men would produce wine with the fall harvest of grapes and store it in large wooden casks in the basements of their homes. At dinnertime, someone would be sent to fill the carafe with wine for dinner, and children could get a little wine with water to accompany their meals. During the Christmas holidays, the women would prepare a rich *torta di ciocollata* or chocolate torte, a rich buttery crust filled with melted chocolate or a *torta di riso*, a rice-filled sweet pastry.

Commercial firms baked the crusty Italian bread; but early on, the *paisani* in Connecticut would have to travel to a larger city to purchase the loaves, reminders them of home, or their specialty cold cuts, the opposites of American baloney. As the diet expanded so did the family members. Age and good nutrition brought portliness to the once thin women, and since excess weight was a sign of wealth, they did not worry about the accumulation.

The religious holidays were celebrated with Mass and long, calorie-rich, multi course dinners for all the families. Dora would be an avid church attendee, but Bill would make an appearance on the major holidays since he would keep his business open on Christmas, Easter and Thanksgiving mornings for those who might have forgotten some item. Friday meant sacrifice since it was a sin to eat meat on that day. Going to confession was not a pleasant experience for Dora, since she did not understand the ritual or the language well enough to hear the priestly admonitions or to confess her venial sins.

One of the relatives had explained the difference between the deadly mortal sins and the relatively minor venial ones, and Dora had decided on the latter since she had neither the time nor inclination to commit the former. The men had brought their anti-clerical attitudes from the old country where Church and State were always at odds. Religion was an add-on for these Italians, going to church an insurance policy against the fires of hell. Italians, schooled and unschooled, had heard of Dante's *Inferno* and no one wanted to take any chances.

The Spinach Wars

The toothless, kerchiefed woman
in black attire hovers over the fidgeting child
with eggs and freshly squeezed oranges
and nods her head in despair.

"Mangia,mangia, piccola bestia"
"Eat, eat you little rascal."
She scurries around the kitchen,
soiled apron, gray hair flying.

She empties the larder as
to tempt this skinny kid,
only Italian child who won't eat.
Who wrinkles her nose in defiance.

Shame, shame on these immigrants,
new to this land of plenty.
Those who drool over plates of edibles
and lick their plates clean.

What kind of child is this
distrustful, disobedient, devilish?
She who tests the mettle of the clan
relishing leary looks and sighs.

She cuts her teeth on these daily wars.
The more they try to stuff, mold her
the more prickly she becomes,
rebellious American brat.

The spinach battles rage daily.
Fresh leaves rinsed in icy water
Cooked, smothered in olive oil are
force fed-then a late night vomit.
The brutal sixteen-year war ended
without a truce, tears, tantrums.
No bloody battlefield or no man's land
Spent parents send Hera off to school.

Peace at last.   Peace at last.

gm hanson

Chapter 7
Expanding the family

*A*s the country bounced around from worse to better to bad, the citizens coped as well as they could during the late thirties and early forties while old enemies collided and new alliances were formed in the rest of the world. While the Spanish were engaged in their own civil war, the other European countries were in ferment.

In 1936 Hitler renounced the Locarno Pact that had guaranteed European country borders and entered into anti-Communist pacts with Japan and Italy. Italy then invaded Ethiopia, and China and Japan began their own war. 1937 saw the seeds of the problems in the Middle East bear fruit as the Arabs revolted against the Jews in Palestine, resulting in a partitioning of the country in 1947 by the Royal Commission.

In the United States, unemployment was at 16.9% as the economy floundered and Dust Bowl problems persisted for American agriculture. Roosevelt was re-elected by a wide margin, and he attempted to build and expand programs and projects in order to put Americans back to work. The Hoover Dam was completed, and the United States developed the B-17 bomber, expanding US military might. Standard Oil discovered the black gold in Saudi Arabia thereby increasing United States interest in foreign policy, particularly in the Middle East. Now that part of the world became more than a fascination with the exotic culture since money was to be made and United States interests preserved.

Despite the hardships and the hurricane of 1938 that devastated many homes and businesses along the northeast coast, Americans would escape into movies such as "Gone With the Wind", "Casablanca" or radio dramas as scary as the "War of the Worlds." Bing Crosby would lull them into believing in an American "White Christmas," and Frank Sinatra began to croon his love songs. All these forms of escape gave people the hope to go on and set aside their fears and anxieties, albeit for a moment.

Dora worried about her parents in Italy since the Axis powers were swallowing countries in Europe: first Austria, then Poland, Bohemia, Moravia, Denmark, the Netherlands, Belgium, France and Luxembourg. The Nazis were destroying Jewish shops, homes and synagogues, and according to some reports, sending people to concentration camps where all sorts of abuses were committed against men, women and children. Dora had heard that Mussolini and his government were going along with Hitler. She was horrified that her homeland would align with such a man, a *matto* or crazy man, who could only make the trains run on time but who had become a dictator and a sycophant of the Germans.

World War II formally began in 1939, but Americans had become more isolationists after World War I and did not want to meddle in European affairs. Dora could hardly believe the stories she heard about the Jews. She had heard all of the stereotypical talk about how Jews loved money, but she could not understand why German Nazis would want to exterminate these people. She learned that her father Alessio had hidden a trunk in his home filled with the belongings of a Jewish family from Lucca, as they tried to flee the Nazis.

In nearby villages, priests and villagers risked their lives to hide Jewish children from the Nazis and Fascists, those Italians who sympathized with Hitler. When Dora went to the movies, she saw pictures of the high-stepping Nazi soldiers marching as Hitler urged them on to purify the motherland and extend their power over the neighbors who had humiliated them after the First World War. She trembled as she watched these harsh pictures and hoped that they would never march in her country and sweep up her neighbors, the Savages, who owned the butcher shop near Danielson Fruit.

There was talk that Roosevelt's administration was trying to help the Jewish people, but she could not understand why the government had turned away thousands of Jewish immigrants trying to enter this country. Things did not make sense to her simple understanding of world affairs she learned about from radio broadcasts and comments from the males in the family. Her husband said that America would be obliged to go to war at some point since he believed that the Europeans could not go it alone.

"Must human beings always be at war?" Dora thought, remembering that for most of her life in Italy and America she had known war from a distance.

Meanwhile, President Roosevelt submitted a $1,319-million dollar defense budget while declaring neutrality. In 1940, he signed the Selective Service Act authorizing conscription; and in the following year, he used his power to lease war supplies to other countries. It seemed that the nation was preparing to defend their way of life against the Nazis and the Japanese, both of whom were waging war on nearby countries. How could the United States remain safe with these encroaching, aggressive armies and navies on the march?

Then, on December 7, 1941 Japan launched a surprise attack on the U.S.fleet at Pearl Harbor thereby bringing the United States into World War II. Out of fear and trepidation, the government interred more than 120,000 Japanese or citizens of Japanese ancestries in relocation centers. Fear and paranoia were gripping the nation. Quietly, the government initiated and supported the "Manhattan Project" to design and build the atomic bomb, a powerful weapon developed by expatriate German, Italian and American scientists. These years saw expanded discoveries in the medical and physical sciences because America was considered the leader in research, both peaceful and not so peaceful, saving lives and taking them.

Food and weapons were sent to Britain under the Lend-Lease Act. Unemployment in the United States that had been as high as 19% in 1938 slipped to 9.9% in 1941 and would go as low as 1.2% in 1944 as Americans were reluctantly preparing to sacrifice again. The crisis brought all people together to fight their common enemies.

During these war years, the Italian families and all immigrant groups sat close to their radios to hear news of their embattled countries. They sent clothes to families in the villages and waited for letters to re-assure themselves of the safety of their relatives and former neighbors. Americans were united behind the war effort, but the immigrant families could not help but worry. News did not travel fast so the waiting and wondering was unbearably intense, especially for Dora who felt helpless to aid her elderly parents. She worried about the lack of food and whether soldiers would take over her village and kill the inhabitants suspected of any kind of collaboration with the Allies or with Jews.

Finally, in July of 1943, Mussolini was deposed and placed under arrest. This was some consolation to the immigrant families, but they knew that many battles were yet to be fought throughout Europe before any peace was achieved since Germans had invaded their former ally resulting in Italy becoming a battlefield for the remainder of the war.

On April 25, 1945 American troops liberated Italy. Dora was both relieved and proud of her new homeland. She and Bill loved to play "God Bless America" sung by Kate Smith on the RCA phonograph they had purchased last year and muddled along in their broken English accents. The needle had to be frequently changed since they loved listening to their music: Italian opera and folk songs sung by Enrico Caruso, Carlo Bergonzi and Giusieppe di Stefano.

To celebrate, Bill took Dora to see "Casablanca" in the big city of Providence, Rhode Island. She would slip out of her flowered housedress and don a muted grey long skirt and tunic top together with a matching hat, gloves and purse. Nude colored nylon stockings covered her legs that would sit comfortably in high-heeled black shoes. It was such a treat to go to the movies in a new place and be escorted by her handsome husband who dressed in a dark suit, shirt and tie and a classic men's hat.

Meanwhile, life in the small towns of America was bustling. Everyone was working, sacrificing; victory gardens were a popular way to get fresh food as most people received a rationing of stamps for meat, butter and other staples while bananas were like gold. Dora and Bill were fortunate to own a grocery store so their diet remained unchanged, but they did barter with the Jewish butcher, Morris Savage, who owned the shop next door. Everyone who could afford to bought US

Savings Bonds to support the troops and the war effort as Americans took pride in the uniformed soldiers and sailors walking around town while on leave. Americans of all colors, classes and cultures united.

In 1943, a new policy allowed the withholding of taxes on wages that would help subsidize government expenses. Rumors of German submarines off the coast of New York City frightened citizens, as did the threat of Japanese Kamikaze pilots in the skies off the California coast. Blackouts would be called to fool the enemy so they could not see their targets; and during those dark nights, families would cover the windows and sit by candlelight and talk, reminding Dora of the darkness in her Riolo home where sundown meant shadows, stillness and early bedtimes.

In 1943 when the Allies invaded Normandy, Dora's brother, Alfeo, from St. Louis and his wife, Lola, came to help Bill and Dora in the business since Dora was pregnant and needed relief from her many jobs. Lola came from a family of distant relatives living in Riolo.

She was born in the United States, one of seven children born to Alessio's cousin, Letizia. Lola was a beautiful, dark-haired woman of 23 when she accompanied her husband to Connecticut. She had never left home and was very close to her tightly knit family in Missouri, loved to sing in church with a beautiful soprano voice and have fun with the children.

She would make banana splits for her niece and nephew during the blackouts and sing songs to them to allay their fears. A good trooper, she would work in the grocery store and beguile the customers with her verbosity and her good looks. When she dressed in her black dress and pink short jacket to attend church, she would attract the stares of both women and men and made people wonder how Alfeo, a somewhat staid and serious man, had attracted such a beauty? She was a welcome addition to the serious women of the Lucchesi family.

The men had avoided war service for the most part, but one of the extended family members, Aldo Cassettari, was wounded during the invasion of Normandy. He was sent home with shrapnel and painful memories embedded in his head, never the same man. He needed attention and caring, and Wanda, Arimede and Melba's daughter, provided that security. The family embraced him, and tried to support him in any way they could, by providing a job and their affection; but he would carry the pain of those days in the war zone with him throughout his life. The men in the families were proud of his service but relieved that they had dodged the bullet.

Bill and Dora settled into the new home they had bought a few months before the arrival of Lola and Alfeo. The house was in a residential area of town near public grade and high schools; however, a rubber plant was down the street making it a less fashionable area— fine for immigrants and middle class families like teachers, small business owners, ministers and mill workers. The wealthier families lived on the outskirts of town on streets with names like Peckham Lane or Broad Street.

There were numerous evergreens in the yard of their new home, a pear tree outside a bedroom window and irises, lilies of the valley and violets in the flowerbeds. It was a corner property house with two-stories and two apartments on the second floor. A large forsythia bush bordered the front entrance by the screened in porch. In the back of the building there was a rectangular opening in the brick of the lower section of the house that was set aside for pets or animals, forbidden entrance into the living quarters. Clotheslines, high enough to avoid hitting when walking in the yard but low enough to reach when hanging out the weekly wash, stretched from a hook on the house to a pole near the retaining wall.

Two vertical doors that had to be swung open to gain entrance shuttered the stairs leading down to the cellar. In that cellar were steps leading up to the first floor apartment, a large coal bin to feed an imposing grey, hungry furnace and a raised dais for a washing machine. The street was named Cottage Street, but there were no cottages, only large multifamily homes in various sizes and colors.

It was to be an investment home for Dora and Bill making them landlords in addition to being business owners. Life was looking good. Lola and Alfeo occupied one bedroom at the Cottage Street entrance to the house while Gloria occupied a smaller room near her parents' bedroom. The kitchen, a large room with a sculpted wooden table topped by a sliding metal top, and a credenza, nestled near the bathroom and pantry.

The adjoining living room functioned as a gathering place for children and adults who wanted to listen to the radio and enjoy the comedies of Jack Benny, the scary programs of "The Shadow" or the trials and tribulations of the daytime drama heroine, Stella Dallas. The fantasy world of the movies or radio programs saved Americans from total despair.

Dora and Bill had inherited tenants, one of whom was a spinster named Rose Weaver while the Perraults, Harriet and Eddie, occupied the larger apartment at the front of the house. They were friendly and cordial, and Bill was happy with the timely rent payments. He had paid cash for the apartment house so he needed the extra money to keep the home heated and maintained, the encircling lawn cut, trees and bushes trimmed and structures painted. Someone had to pay the coal delivery man, the milkman, the iceman and the handyman.

Keeping up a house was not easy since someone had to go down into the dark cellar and shovel coal into the furnace and keep the place free of coal dust. All family members over the age of six had to participate in that activity. Pressure was building in the family as life had become more complicated.

By May of 1945, the Axis was in retreat. With Hitler's suicide, Germany surrendered, and the Allies turned their full attention to Japan. Everyone celebrated the end of the war and remembered where they were and what they were doing when President Roosevelt made the announcement on the radio.

In May 1943, Dora was driven to Day Kimball Hospital in Putnam just in time to deliver a 7 pound 9 ounce boy. Bill was on a trip to the market, and when he arrived at home, his brothers were waiting.

"Congratulations," said Arimede," you are the proud father of a beautiful little girl."

Bill could hardly believe what he heard. He needed a son to carry on the family name and take over the business since he doubted that a girl would be interested in the grocery store. After all, women would marry and end up cooking and washing diapers.

"Oh no, I'm leaving town. What was she thinking? She knew I wanted a son."

Arimede and Elside pulled out a couple of expensive Cuban cigars and laughed gleefully.

"Here, Bill, have a cigar. You can stay. Dora had a boy, so relax. We won't tell the little princess what you said. Let's go up and see the baby Prince."

They hopped into Arimede's car and sped to the hospital as they left a trail of brown smoke drifting out the windows of the old blue Studebaker. The blonde, blue-eyed boy was already holding court with a coterie of uncles, aunts and cousins gazing through the nursery window and breathing a sigh of relief that a son had been born and would be named William Peter Lucchesi. The Prince had arrived, and the family rejoiced. Exhausted and oblivious, Dora slept peacefully in her hospital room as the celebration went on outside.

Little Ronnie Perrault was born on the same day, in the same hospital, and both mothers returned to 49 Cottage Street four days later. Friends and relatives oohed and ahhed upon their arrival. Aunt Lola was particularly enchanted with the new baby and immediately bonded, offering to feed, diaper and hold the little one.

She wondered whether she would ever have children of her own so thought she had better enjoy this one. He was a welcome relief to her niece, Gloria, who seemed to become brattier and more outspoken every day. Lola herself had not found her voice, having been a respectful and considerate child and young woman. Being one of many, Lola had learned to be quiet and keep her ideas and feelings to herself.

As she combed Gloria's hair and spun out the banana curls, she would admonish and warn the child, "Be still and watch your tongue, little girl, because you are going to be in for big trouble with your parents, especially now that you have a little brother."

"What difference will he make? He is small, always sleeping and doesn't talk. I don't know what all the fuss is about," responded the soon-to-be deposed princess.

There was plenty of fuss in the world when Bill, Jr. arrived, and the family would turn their gaze outward towards that world once the initial excitement of a new boy subsided. The war against Japan had not yet been won, and all Americans held a slim glimmer of hope that the final chapter would be written soon. On August 6 and 9, 1945, the United States dropped atomic bombs on the cities of Hiroshima and Nagasaki, and despite the preservation of American lives, the victory was bittersweet because the toll of these attacks shattered America's self-image as a moral conqueror.

The Night Before Christmas—in Connecticut

Creeping along the cold linoleum floor
The child inches towards the lights on the
Christmas tree—red   green   white   blue
flicker in syncope. The electric train
sits quietly awaiting the switch.
The caboose trails the other cars
With names like Northern Pacific,
Bethlehem Steel.

Tinsel hanging haphazardly
glows and reflects the light while
ornaments fake snow slowly sway
on the green fir branches.

The quiet stillness of this Christmas eve,
broken only by the child's heavy breathing ,
panting anticipation

She can't wait for Christmas morn
can"t share the limelight with
little brother who focuses the doting
parental eyes on himself
as he rips and tears, squeals, seduces.

She embarks on this lonely mission,

check out "just a few presents."
Quietly pulling the scotch tape ends, she
releases the box out of its colorful wrap.

"Wow, gee, I can't believe this is for me."
A golden heart-shaped locket dangling
on wheat chain.
"No brother of mine will want this."
She sighs in relief,reluctantly
Returns it to its pristine state.

"Only one more, only one more."
Cries the little sneak in red pajamas.
She pulls out another box from the pile,
hears a noise, a pattering of feet outside
On the roof? On the porch?

Could it be? Santa? Reindeer?
"Oh, my, hurry, I'll find
coal in my stocking."

She scurries back to her bed, pulls
covers over her head, sighing in relief
to await the dawn's early light.

gm hanson

Danielson Fruit   1945

Bill and Gloria   1939

Gloria and Billy 1943

Chapter 8
Post-war Travel

*T*he post-war life in the United States remained in the growth mode as nations and citizens struggled to return to normalcy after years of war and sacrifice. Americans, their allies and their former enemies wanted a respite from the horrors accompanying the conflicts of the early twentieth century. Fyodor Dostoevsky, the great Russian writer, predicted the slaughter of the twentieth century when men who thought their ideas and ideals were better than those of other men and would annihilate the outsiders so that humankind would somehow be better.

Could human beings ever live in peace? How could they learn to live in harmony? One response of the world community was the establishment of the United Nations where countries might learn to settle their differences with representatives sitting around a table and no guns in sight. Another remarkable consequence of western leaders' policies was the Nuremberg trials scene ending in the conviction of twelve Nazi leaders. "Enough brutality and genocide, give us an end or at least a respite."

Despite these positive signs, Winston Churchill, the prime minister of England, saw storm clouds on the horizon and warned of Soviet expansion. The Cold War began –one brief year following the end of World War ll. The planet was heating up again as the Soviet Union rejected the US plan for UN atomic-energy control in 1947, and in response President Harry Truman proposed a doctrine in Congress to contain Communist expansion.

There was peace in some parts of the world: Italy, Romania, Bulgaria and Hungary found some semblance of order and harmony. Italy struggled to oust the monarchy and establish a democracy, aligning itself with the United States and its Marshall Plan, an economic recovery package designed to help Italy and other European countries rebuild after the war. Consequently, Americans felt safe to visit their ancestral homelands.

Bill had been experiencing stomach problems for a few years and decided to "take the waters" in Italy to regain his health. Spas and mineral water springs were popular in Europe and in the United States to treat various disorders and to assist individuals regain their vitality.

Dora was only too happy to take a trip to her homeland and visit her parents; and she was delighted that Bill's brother, Elside, decided to go along since his wife, Mini, had not seen her mother, Caterina, in many years. Caterina had lived with her sister, Celestina, and her brother-in-law, Egisto, in a house near Vittoria and Alessio's since her husband, Armando, had died prematurely. Caterina and Celestina were cousins of Alessio Prosperi and close neighbors.

Danielson Fruit would be in the hands of Dora's brother, Emo and his wife, Prima, who had moved from St. Louis to take the job and live in the Lucchesi home. Their daughter, Silvana, a lively, attractive woman in her twenties, went to work as a maid to Melba who had developed crippling arthritis. All details had been worked out, and everything was in place for a win-win situation for everyone.

The members of both families boarded the "Sobieski," an 11,030 gross ton ship that became an Allied troop vessel in 1939 and returned to its owners, the Gdyndia-American Line, in 1947 to transport passengers from Europe to New York. The accommodations included 70 first class units, 270 cabins and 600 tourist rooms.

The Lucchesi families occupied adjoining cabins enjoying a porthole view. The ship was fitted with large dining rooms segregated by class, deck chairs, shuffleboard areas and a swimming pool. Once settled into the small cabin, Gloria and her cousin, Nancy, left their parents to unpack and settle down while they toured the ship. They made their plans to escape their overseers and have a good time. Since Dora and Mini became seasick shortly after leaving New York, they could not easily check on their children since Bill was then entrusted with his four-year-old son, Billy, who required constant supervision thereby leaving Gloria and Nancy free to roam.

"Boy, is this going to be fun", exclaimed Gloria, who at eleven was sprouting bigger wings to flap along with her assertive tongue.

"Well, let's be careful. We don't want to get into trouble," responded the cautious Nancy who, despite being one year older than her cousin was more of a follower than a leader. She was a pretty girl with a round face, blue eyes and a winsome smile who was indulged by her overprotective and anxious mother. As an only child she longed to be part of a pair or a group—a perfect foot soldier for her generalissimo cousin.

"Let's check out the pool and the food and see if there are any other kids on this boat.," exclaimed Gloria as she took Nancy's hand and led her up the steps to the main deck.

They ran up and down the deck and watched the ocean waves and the darkening sky, the sun retreating in the west, the clouds, rolling in as the graceful 511-foot ship cut through the waves on its way to Genoa. The eight-day trip was filled with adventures for some passengers; particularly the young ones who played shuffleboard, ping-pong, swam in the pool and played hide and seek from each other and their parents. Gloria and Nancy did not know how to swim so they made their way clutching the sides of the pool or flapping their arms as they kept their feet planted firmly on the stairs or the shallow end.

Not quite in their teens, Gloria and Nancy were beginning to experience stirrings of their sexuality, as were the pre-pubescent boys in the pool taunting and teasing all the girls in sight. One of them swam over to Gloria and pulled her away from the wall saying, "Com' on, chicken, swim to the other side. Let's race."

"I'm drowning, I'm drowning," Gloria screamed as she gulped and gagged, doggy paddled and kicked her way to the safety of the wall, to catch her breath. She spied her dad out of the corner of her eye as he came upon the scene and witnessed his struggling daughter, but he felt helpless to do much since he had never learned how to swim. He was stuck in place and speechless, and before he could summon help he heard her voice.

Fearing his disapproval, she yelled out to him, "Dad, Dad, I know how to swim! I know how to swim!" She had become a master of the detour, and this time the little maneuver kept her out of trouble.

Bill had also learned the art of diversion. While Dora was below deck putting Bill, Jr. for a nap, Bill, Sr. was looking at the ladies, flirting and reverting to his bachelor behavior.

"Harmless enough," he told his brother who questioned him.

"I don't think it's as harmless as you think. You don't want to follow in Arimede's footsteps, especially in Italy where the women are vulnerable. Do you want to embarrass your wife in Riolo where everyone knows everyone else's business?"

"You are assuming that I am going to take this behavior to Riolo. I am not."

"Yes, I do, because I see your roving eye and watch your seductive talk, behaviors that won't escape your mother-in-law's hawkish eyes. Vittoria will kill you or have you killed if you bring shame on her family. Remember, she was not someone you could charm so easily."

The clouds were thickening on the horizon, and the smell of betrayal was already in the air.

Lucchesi families on the Sobiesky   1947

Migration

Sea turtles travel thousands of miles
to return yearly to their natal homes.
Risking adversity, they swim, towards
familiar smells and sands, led on by
who knows what geomagnetic field.

Human migrants long to find home,
not feed or hatch but to connect.
Despite hardship they seek comfort,
discovery and roots to birth sites.
Neither moon nor sun lead the way,

Only love.

gm hanson

Chapter 9
Cultural Changes

*T*he trip from Genoa to Bagni di Lucca, a beautiful river town close to Lucca and Pisa in Tuscany, was long but manageable; however, the trek up the mountain to the village was interminably long and barely doable for these Americans accustomed to sidewalks and automobiles. The dirt paths had been well trodden by villagers, soldiers and visitors and consisted of a hilly ascent with few places to stop and rest, The Stone Barn or Capanna de Mattoni providing fresh water and a place to sit. The mule carried the suitcases, but bags and satchels were the responsibility of the walkers who, at that point, were tired, thirsty and irritable.

Dora and Mini walked behind their husbands and carried most of the extra baggage while Bill and Elside took turns carrying little Billy on their shoulders and talking to the owner of the donkey. The rest stop at the small shrine of the Blessed Virgin Mary could not have come any sooner. They could sit in the shade and munch on some bread and salami bought in town and drink with heads bent and wide-open mouths at the fountain nearby.

Dora and Mini would moan about how much they missed being driven around in an automobile, and they both knew what lay ahead for them in the village, living the old life of survival. In addition to the hardships of daily life, they would have the burden of hovering over their daughters—who thought they were ready to flee the nest but were still totally unaware of what lay ahead.

"We will have to watch these girls of ours," warned Mini who had noticed how Nancy and Gloria were getting into some kind of mischief each day. Of course, she knew that the younger cousin was the instigator of any trouble despite the frequent spankings and admonitions she received from her father. Her own daughter, Nancy, was quiet and demure; but when she played with her cousin, she would be more than happy to pursue a life of adventure and challenge in an environment that provided many hiding places from mothers busy with chores.

"Oh yes, I didn't see much during the ocean voyage because of my seasickness, but what I did see was a little sparkle in their eyes when boys were around. I think we will have our hands full with these little rascals."

The welcoming committee was out in the *piazza* or town center when the weary travelers arrived since Vittoria and Alessio had heard from Pinzino, the town gossip, that his friend, the mule driver, was going to meet the Americani. The proud grandparents had spread the word, and all the villagers, mostly older women who had been left behind in the great migration west had ended their chores early so they could congregate and embrace the visitors.

After much kissing and hugging, the weary travelers made their way to the grandparents' homes. Elside and his family were swept along to Caterina's home while Bill and his family climbed another hill along stone-cobbled streets to Vittoria and Alessio's modest stone house where the smell of dinner cooking brought instant relief.

Dora knew her way around the kitchen and proceeded to help her mother prepare the meal. Vittoria
was in good spirits and had prepared pasta, *necchi* or
pancakes, and sausage, expecting everyone to devour
her dinner with delight, but she was not prepared to
watch the fussy eater in the group who did not like the
pancakes made with chestnut flour and who had folded
it in her lap so she could discard it later. Nothing escaped the eagle eye of her grandmother, Vittoria, who
quickly chastised both mother and child. The uneasy
truce between mother and daughter had ended, and the
battle between grandmother and grandchild had just
begun.

After dinner, they walked to the home belonging to
Dora's brother, Emo, where they would spend the year.
It was a newly built house in the middle part of town.
Marble floors at the lower level gave way to a veranda
overlooking the valley in the Apennine mountain range.
A small cubicle with a narrow door occupied one corner
of this outside porch-- this was the outhouse. Two bedrooms were on the second floor, each with a bed, a bedpan at the foot of the bed, a ceramic bowl on a stand
with a vase of water nearby and a chest of drawers. The
dining room and kitchen occupying the first floor, were
minimally decorated, a long wooden table and chairs in
the eating area and a prep table, rinsing sink area and
fireplace in the adjoining kitchen. Marble steps con-
nected these two floors while a double door led out to
the veranda.

Beneath the house was the open area where farm
tools and hay were stored, and cages for rabbits nestled
in the corner. Near the entrance of the house was a
fenced-in area where a pig, several chickens and one
rooster resided.

The garden was terraced with areas for fruits and

vegetables: grapes and fruit trees like pear, apple or fig, displaying their glory and long lines of tilled soil for tomatoes, zucchini and potatoes. At the end of the garden was a wide stone, rectangular pool or *pozzo* with running cold water and a washboard stone where the women would scrub the family clothes after having made a *"bollito"* of steaming hot water, ashes and burlap over the fireplace. Not much had changed since Dora's departure for the New World.

All looked comfortable and convenient in the light of day. Dora and Bill knew what to expect, but their daughter was in for a rude awakening, cold marble floors, bedrooms without heat and outdoor toilet, standard for village life at the time but a whole new world for an American child. Nights were scary times for them since the darkness was thick and black or a moon would appear and create ghostly shadows on the walls and floors. Days were to be laced with chores, and it seemed that childhood had been tucked away in storage.

"Why do I have to go to the fountain to get water for coffee? I don't drink coffee. Why do I have to collect sticks and carry them on my head to start the fire? Why should I get my own breakfast egg from the chicken coop? Why, Why, Why?"

Dora would answer in the only way she knew how, "This is how it's done here. Children must help out, and these are your jobs. In fact, tomorrow morning you will get the goat's milk from the next village before you go to school."

"What? Goat's milk? How far is the next village? Before school?"

"Quiet, Gloria, you don't want your father to hear you complain."

"I want to go back home. Why did you take me to

this ugly place?"

Father wouldn't hear because he was usually roaming about the village visiting old friends, hunting with his buddies or playing cards in the piazza. The women would cook, clean, wash, bake, mend and iron during the daylight hours and fall into their beds exhausted from the day's survival routine. It was the perfect birth control device since they were fast asleep when husbands came in from their roaming, but on the other hand, this lifestyle did not do much to bring couples together.

The roles were ingrained in Bill and Dora, and the separation grew. Bill became a harsher disciplinarian, especially of his daughter who had begun to notice boys and wanted to be out and about with her friends. On many occasions he would take a thin branch from an olive tree and switch her legs when she had disobeyed.

His temper seemed to flare more than usual the older she became. Was the memory of his father's beatings triggering these outbursts? Vittoria thought the girl deserved the switch, but Alessio believed that these punishments were too harsh. Dora sided with her father most of the time since she saw how Bill could be an understanding and loving parent on some social occasions.

The village dances held in the community hall usually celebrated religious holidays. While accordion music played dance tunes, Dora would sit on the sidelines watching as her husband twirled with his daughter in a *quadrilla*, a square dance or slow dance with the pretty, thin women who would attend from the neighboring towns. Sharing his American cigarettes and impressing them with his worldly demeanor, he was the hit of the party. Vittoria would glare, and the older women would whisper as Dora kept her thoughts and feelings to herself. She would watch her children and pray that the evening would end before she would melt with embarrassment and anger.

All of this rejection from her once-attentive husband was a shock to her. Granted she had gained weight since the birth of her children, but she thought she kept herself well groomed and attractive. It seems that Bill did not see her in that way since he became distant and dismissive of her entreaties. She thought she had been a good wife, worker, partner, mother and caretaker, responding to his every whim; cooking him special food, ironing his clothes just so and delivering his coffee to him after dinner. She even stirred it for him.

What was she to do? She was unsure whether her husband would stay with her or seek another wife or mistress. She had heard that Bill's brother, Arimede, was involved with an Italian woman who remained his lover for many years despite his infrequent visits to Italy.

She decided to keep her suspicions to herself until she went back home to the States. Then she would confide in her sister-in-law, Dina, who would give her wise counsel and perhaps intercede with her brother. Knowing that she could confide in only one person in this wide world left her feeling alone and lonely. Was this her destiny? She had once heard that the old Roman philosopher Lucretius counsel: "Limit your wants, and you will limit the pain of not getting so trim your wants to avoid suffering." Is that what she should do? She had little education, could barely speak her adopted country's language and had two young children. She felt her life caving in around her, and avoided her mother who kept glancing at her and looking as if she was saying, "I told you so."

Life in this village of post-war Italy was not easy for anyone, particularly women who bore the heavy burden of gathering—wood, water, food and dirty clothes. Children would venture forth early in the morning for a thirty minute walk to the one room school house in Monti di Villa while the women did the assigned tasks for that particular day: Monday was laundry day, Tuesday was baking bread in the communal oven, and Wednesday, Thursday, Friday, Saturday were devoted to cleaning, preparing food or feeding the animals.

Sunday was by no means a day of rest since meals had to be prepared and dishes and pots and pans scrubbed after attending Mass in the Church of St. Nicola in the town square. The women would be lucky to sit down for a card game of *"Briscola"* with their families. Dora was resigned to this role as she tried to please everyone and hold dignity to herself before her parents, relatives, friends and villagers.

Her husband's regimen for "taking the waters" at the spa in Montecatini or the baths in Bagni di Lucca where he hoped to quell the fire and distress in his belly kept her near. She would pray to St, Jude, the saint of lost causes while noticing out of the corner of her eye that her daughter would stare at her father and follow him around. Would an eleven-year-old suspect these things or was she trying to avoid "women's work?" Dora ached to get home-life was much easier in Danielson, Connecticut, USA.

"Bide your time, bide your time," she crooned.

Sheets in the Wind

Mother and daughter in a two step
Stretching the sundrenched sheets

Pull, pull   fold in half
Pull, pull again   fold in quarters

Stepping in   hands touching
Stepping back   tugging the cloth

Warm breeze and fond memories

gmhanson

Chapter 10
The Return

"H ome at last, home at last," Dora and Gloria sighed in unison once they stepped off the ship in New York City. Bill and Billy were less delighted since the village life was good for little boys and their dads on holiday. The welcoming party in Danielson was an occasion for a family gathering with all the relatives bringing food while the travelers gave small gifts to the children and good Italian delicacies to the adults.

The exhausted families fell into their warm beds, near their bathrooms with running hot and cold water. Gloria could hardly contain herself when she awoke, running around the house turning on faucets and flushing toilets and thinking she was now in heaven. She was sure. "*Paradiso, Paradiso,*" she would sing, showing off her mastery of Italian.

Dora soon returned to her routine house and store work. Her brother, Emo, and his wife, Prima, had kept the apartment impeccably clean, and now they would live together until the St. Louis couple decided on their next move. Having another woman in the house made it easier for Dora since Prima was an excellent cook, although an anxious one, who taught her sister-in-law how to prepare many delicious dishes for each evening meal.

Prima was from a different province so her culinary

dishes were different than the ones Dora had experienced. Prima communicated everything verbally so Dora learned to pay attention and be the quiet sous chef as she gained her stripes in the kitchen. Their delicious tortes made them popular with family and Gloria's friends who would gather to get a slice of *torta di ciocollata* or chocolate torte. Her best friend, Harvey Egan, asked Mrs. Lucchesi to adopt him to reap the benefits of this Italian kitchen.

The nineteen fifties began with the Cold War still raging and the United States becoming a leader in the development of more powerful weapons of mass destruction. By 1953 a new president, Dwight Eisenhower, heralded a new era of peace and prosperity while warning Americans of the dangers of the military-industrial complex. Unemployment was at 3% in 1953, and with the Korean War ending, Americans thought they might enjoy living the American dream. Even the comedians of that era turned away from satire to a gentler humor mirroring the domestic life or creating "Who's on First," made famous by Abbott and Costello. Bill and Dora certainly looked with pride at their accomplishments: a house, automobile, a black and white television, a stable business, and two healthy children.

Dora looked out her kitchen window at her daughter walking to school and saw herself as a young girl trudging up the hill to her one room schoolhouse in Monti di Villa. She lingered in that image savoring the smell of the woods and the sound of the leaves crackling beneath her feet. Coming back to reality she pondered her life. Here she was, a forty-two-year old illiterate immigrant woman who was leading a life of work and responsibility.

Her childhood had been interrupted by her passion for a man who now ignored and dismissed her. She felt like a beast of burden whose only function was to carry the load and care for everyone. She felt a twinge of envy for her young daughter who had the world wide open before her and who seemed to have some innate knowledge of the importance of self reliance and selfishness in order to forge her own identity. Perhaps she has learned these lessons by watching my struggle, Dora thought to herself.

In keeping with the promise to seek the advice of her friend and sister-in-law, she guided Dina into the kitchen as the husbands puffed away on cigars in the living room while watching the daily news and stock market reports.

"Dina, I don't know what to do. Your brother shuns me, and I think he is seeing other women behind my back. In Italy, he was always flirting with the young ones in the village. He would say he was going hunting and return way after dark. Now he leaves in the afternoon to make deliveries but doesn't re-appear for hours. I feel so angry and powerless. What am I to do?"

"Bill has always had an eye for the women. He and Arimede were prowling around after girls when they were selling statues on the road. Many Italian men learned these ways when they were young and here alone, away from family and friends, while others are born that way. It's bred in their bones. I don't know what you can do to stop this, but I will speak to Elside, and ask him to try to talk some sense into your husband. He is a good man, loyal to his wife and a serious family member."

"I appreciate your help. I am so worried that I am eating too much to quell that pain in my belly and my heart. That doesn't help either since my weight gain does not make me a desirable woman, I fear. I look in the mirror and see a fat woman with dumpy looking clothes and the sagging face of an old woman."

"You are fine just the way you are. Bill could not have found another loyal, tenacious and generous person as yourself."

Several days later, the brotherly conversation took place; but alas, amid denials and recriminations, Bill stayed his course thereby eroding the bonds with his siblings and his wife. Soon, however, his ever active gut and deteriorating health would intervene and keep him close to home, making him ever more reliant on his loyal wife who continued to shower him with care and love. She certainly was a lesson in perseverance, a woman who could see herself in those tragic heroines of her favorite soap operas.

As the nuclear families coalesced around living the American dream, they faced the challenges of identity, the children of this generation growing to be Americans, wanting American food and language. Bill and Dora, despite their financial success, were now reaping what they had sown. They could not read or write English well enough to be full citizens and Americans since instead of focusing on their own education, they had put all their energies into work and building their business. Now they struggled to integrate and learn the ways of this changing world.

They had to rely on the oral tradition, on what they heard from customers, radio, television or younger family members. Bill's social graces gave him an edge since he could speak to everyone, listen and learn. Dora, on the other hand, relied on television and radio, understanding but unable to translate what she had heard into English. She was at a clear disadvantage and began to realize the depths and consequences of her dependency.

"What comes around, goes around," the saying

goes, and as her mother had done before her, Dora was about to re-visit abandonment by her own daughter, Gloria, who, having been a successful student despite her frequent acts of rebellion against the strict rules of her parents, wanted to leave Connecticut and attend college in another state. Dora could not understand this despite her own history of leaving home. She thought this was different than her situation was in Italy. Why? Why would Gloria want to leave home?

The family had recently moved from the house on Cottage Street in Danielson to a sprawling ranch house in the country, a small, beautiful town, Brooklyn. There was plenty of room for everyone. Gloria could stay at home and attend a local college as her cousin Nancy had done or find a school and hour or so away as cousin Peter and Gloria's best friend, Harvey Egan did.

These children didn't venture too far from the nest. Bill and Dora would buy her a car so she would have independence, but there was no bending of this little branch who was determined to leave the family mass and set out on her own path to independence. Of course, she expected her parents to pay for this flight, but Bill could not say no since he had bragged about his achieving daughter to family, customers and anyone who would listen. How could he say no and save face?

After all, Gloria was not only an excellent student, but the recipient of the Good Citizen award from the Daughters of the American Revolution. This little child of immigrants gave him pride. He had to demonstrate that he supported the American way of letting your children go. He paid the $900.00 annual tuition and room fee with a mixture of joy and sadness.

Proudly, Dora and Bill drove their daughter to New York to drop her off for the first year at the College of New Rochelle, an Ursuline run school in a city that was a twenty-five minute train ride from New York City. Once they arrived, they entered another world of upwardly mobile Roman Catholic parents who drove their daughters in big cars and chatted away in perfect English.

The Ursuline nuns greeted the incoming students and parents, but both Gloria and her parents wanted the day to end since they realized that they didn't quite fit. Language barricaded Bill and Dora so they said their good byes and drove back home to Connecticut where they would be safely ensconced in the country. The daughter, too, felt conspicuous and ill at ease; although she had been active socially in high school, she preferred small, mixed groups or being alone. The ebullient, clubby nature of the predominantly Irish lasses overwhelmed her.

For the next four years, she struggled with establishing an identity, her reputation as a good student and friend was not enough to allow her into the inner sanctum of the bridge playing, socializing popular set. She would set off on Saturdays to explore New York City, walking around Broadway, standing for shows and operas and checking out various neighborhoods, including Harlem where she had been warned never to venture.

In the first few years she dated a high school beau who was attending Yale. Despite her parents disapproval of this "wasp" whose parents snubbed their noses at these nouveau riche Italians, Gloria would go to New Haven to visit after having forged a permission note signed by William and Dora Lucchesi mailed while on a trip home the weekend before. If Bill and Dora had known what their plucky daughter was doing on weekends, they would have pulled her out of that "protected" environment.

Meanwhile, Bill and Dora continued to run Danielson Fruit, and thrive. Their young son Bill was an all-American boy, preferring sports to scholarly pursuits thereby driving his father to distraction. He had wanted his son to be educated and enter one of the professions. They battled on many occasions and would seek advice about what to do about this boy who was sweet and social but not at all interested in the scholastic life, especially since he was reminded daily how he did not measure up to his sister's success.

Despite the comparisons, the two siblings were very close. The big sister who had initially disliked being dethroned became a friend and influencer to her little brother. She would take him to New York City and introduce him to the sights and sounds, the Empire State and United Nations buildings, the subway and the ballgames at Yankee Stadium.

He responded by being her friend and confidant, keeping her secrets, helping her sneak out and guarding her from the eagle eyes of their parents. He was a social being, more like his father than either would admit, but he knew his limitations and his interests; and after attending a boarding school for a year and a local business school for three years, he quit and never looked back. He went to work at a local business and lived at home during his young adulthood.

Bill, Sr. would never accept the discrepancies. He had adopted many of the customs of his new country, but the importance of the "son" in the Italian family was something he could not leave behind. He had projected all of his dreams of professional success on his son, not his daughter

When Gloria asked him for money to attend medical school following college graduation, he refused, saying, "You will just end up washing diapers and never use your training." He would live to regret that statement and carry his guilt to the grave. As a creature of his time, he responded as an Italian male and a protective American father of the fifties.

To Mamma e Pappa

(a la William Carlos Williams)

I'm sorry.

Marry Italian?

Can't do it.

A Gallic bug bit me.

Corned beef and cabbage

Beat out

Pasta and tiramisu.

To Mamma e Pappa

(The longer version)

Sorry I didn't marry Italian
That guy just didn't measure up
He could not hold a candle
to my Irish buttercup.

Wrapped in red and green
such deep brown eyes,
he sang songs of amore
promising binding ties
and years of enduring love.

The dimpled all-American boy
such eyes of greenish blue
Offered simple sonnets
Promising to be true
and years of faithful love.

The Latin lover lit no fire,
only dimming of my senses
A few Irish kisses lit my heart,
burned all of my defenses.

gm hanson

Chapter 11
A New Beginning

*T*he early sixties lit a new fire in Dora's soul. She became a mother-in-law to a young man she adored and admired and also, a grandmother. Gloria had managed to get her own money for graduate school, and while studying Biology she met and married a fellow student, Richard Hanson. Dora had rarely approved of the young men her daughter dated in high school, but this guy was different. Her boyfriends had been local boys, Protestant, from good families but reticent to engage with her or Bill. Richard was good looking, an important quality to Dora, especially since he was also intelligent, polite and respectful.

Since the young couple attended Brown University, a twenty-seven mile drive from Brooklyn, Connecticut, they often would drive to Dora and Bill's for the "best food he had ever tasted in his life." Richard's eyes would roll back into his head following Dora's dinners: the spaghetti sauce and meat balls and soups were to die for, and the pork chops, roasts and steaks were cooked just right. The vegetables from Bill's garden were so fresh and tasty that Richard would swoon with delight.

"I didn't know that food could taste so good until I met Gloria. Dora is the best cook in the world," crowed

Richard who had come from a "it's just fuel" type New Jersey family and gone to college in Boston where he lived on a shoe string and worked as he studied leaving little money or time for good meals. Of course, Dora responded by cooking more food and expanding her repertoire since she had never been praised by anyone for her cooking, or for anything else. Finally, she was getting some recognition at the age of fifty.

A year after marriage, Gloria gave birth to a son, Paul, and Dora and Bill were ecstatic. To have a baby and be needed filled Dora's heart while her days were filled with babysitting for the infant or waiting to baby-sit for the infant. Since Gloria was teaching at a nearby college, she patched together a network for childcare with her mother or her landlady being available to care for the boy while she was at work.

The grandparents were free to drive to Providence to pick up the little bundle since Bill and Dora had sold the business to Arimede's daughter, Wanda and her husband, Aldo. The fact that Gloria had become pregnant again and needed rest and respite made the availability of her parents all the more important. The grandchild pulled the grandparents together like a thread on a spool as their common interest reeled them into the world of the next generation.

The arrival of the second grandson less than a year later was met with mixed joy and sorrow. Little Benjamin was born with clubbed feet requiring surgery and casts that cradled his feet at an angle, this restriction making the infant fussy and needy. Dora wrapped her heart and soul into this child, responding to his every whimper and whine while Bill would care for the oldest grandchild. The family bound together to care for the children allowing Gloria to continue her teaching and Richard to pursue his graduate studies.

These new grandchildren gave Dora and Bill a renewed lease on life--a joyful spirit, a youthful energy and a re-kindling of their vows of devotion and loyalty. Their lives took on a quiet rhythm as they settled into a life of relative peace, prosperity and quiet. The network of family provided avenues for some social life, as relatives were experiencing similar challenges and benefits: sons and daughters married, bore children, and the older generation retired. Since the traveling *nonna* or grandmother Marianna, had died of stomach cancer in 1954, the parents now became the caretakers for their children's children, albeit part-time and with much less power and influence.

Clouds began forming on the horizon as the United States government again sought to extend its influence beyond its shores. Following the untimely death of President John Kennedy, the country was looking at Communist expansion in Vietnam. In 1963 there were 15,000 military advisors in South Vietnam, and in 1964, North Vietnamese torpedoed American destroyers in the Gulf of Tonkin. In response, President Lyndon Johnson ordered retaliation and Congress approved of "any necessary measures" to win in Vietnam. The country braced for another war and another 180,000 American youth were dispatched to fight for "democracy."

Meanwhile, in her small war zone, Dora was fighting the enemy on television. Her son had joined the National Guard, and since the government needed fresh troops, they would be calling for different units to be deployed. When Dora would see Lyndon Johnson on television, she would swear in Italian and begin a tirade at this fool who might take her only son and send him to some "swamp" in the Far East. The losses, potential and real, were beginning to take their toll.

Gloria and Richard had moved to Colorado so that

Richard could complete his Reserve Officers Training Corps commitment in the U.S. Army's Nutrition laboratory in Denver. Dora was devastated by their move since she would lose her "reason for living" in having to let those two little boys out of her world. As a result of the stress during these few years, she lost her low blood pressure and her uterus. She began to feel old and dried up. Only her tears provided the moisture she needed to go on with life.

Falling in Love Again

Holding new life
close to my shriveling breast,
fingers grasp mine
Pull, pull, young, old
Pull, pull don't let go

A blue-eyed bird in a pink ball,
wrapped in a fluffy cloud,
snuggled against my sleeve,
color of a mourning black dove.

Watching the acrid dribble of milk
running down the corner lip,
we taste the first glimmer of decay,
vying with the smell of the old crow.

Licking the pink-skinned forehead
tasting watery sweet, then salty.
This act awakens taste buds
many seconds after the first sip

Smooth, silky, soft, serene,
feeling the heaving chest,
hearing the beating heart,
the old hag feels young,
falls in love once more.

Now and then a shudder,
here and again a gurgle,
a short pleading cry, as
two hearts beat in unison
entwined in bonds of love.

Pull, pull
young and old,
Pull, pull,
don't let go.

gm hanson

Chapter 12
A Reprieve

*T*he clouds lifted when Bill, Jr., married a fellow co-worker, Sandy Palmer, and began his family. They lived nearby so that Dora expected to be closely involved with her new grandchildren. The reality was somewhat different since Sandy, an adopted child, was not interested in forging close family ties with her in-laws, did not want the intrusion of the village life where family members could drop in unannounced and expect weekly family dinners.

Dora and Bill accepted the new situation but did not like it. Their son tried to bridge the gap between wife and parents, but it was difficult and stressful since he was very attached to his parents and wanted frequent contact, even daily communication by phone. Dora coped by shuttling to Philadelphia where her daughter had settled and had borne another child, a girl named Daria.

Previously, Dora had never been so thrilled when girl children arrived since she preferred little boys, but she began to appreciate the females as her daughter showed loyalty and attachment to her parents and insured a close relationship between grandparents and grandchildren. Dora began to acknowledge the benefits of having a daughter in spite of the distance as would Bill who came to appreciate the distaff side of family life and become a doting grandfather.

The late sixties showed more signs of unrest as the civil rights movement had made significant gains thereby upsetting many racists and ordinary citizens who thought that Negroes should know their place. Martin Luther King and Robert Kennedy were both assassinated in 1968 and it seemed that wars in Vietnam and in the streets had brewed political upheaval and a dangerous mix for most Americans.

Richard Nixon, the thirty-seventh President, began the process of Vietnamization in Southeast Asia to tidy up the mess created in that country and give the country back to the people to defend. Despite the signing of the nonproliferation treaty by the United States, Russia and one hundred other countries, there were signals of problems yet to come. China and Russia were at odds, and Libya became an anti-West, pro-Arabic, Islamic republic. These were a few of the clouds on the horizon.

American culture was sowing the seeds of revolution, and the youth of America, coming of age following the anti-war and civil rights movements began to thumb their noses at traditional American mores. "Drugs, sex and rock 'n roll" was the mantra as they gathered in a small upstate New York town called Bethel to celebrate their newly found freedoms. Woodstock was a wake-up call for the rest of America. Times were 'a-changin', and movies like "The Graduate" fueled the hysteria about the loss of morality, tradition and stability.

Many Americans in small towns had been insulated from the initial waves of social changes, but that would soon be altered as their youth would bring them kicking and screaming into this new world. Dora had been a creature of her Italian heritage for most of her life in the United States, and she did not understand all the fuss that the *"neri"* or Negroes were making about their rights. Italians had been discriminated against in this country, and they didn't go out and burn and loot. She had no knowledge of American history so that her thoughts were those garnered from the men in her family or from listening to "Amos 'n' Andy" on the radio. She was not an active racist but a passive, ignorant one. She bore no hatred in her heart, a heart full of love and devotion to her own tribe and one of indifference and misunderstanding to those "others."

Her daughter had threatened to call off her wedding when Bill had refused to allow her graduate student friends who were brown-and black-skinned to attend the ceremony. Bill and Dora thought about it and backed down, but Dora did not understand this daughter of hers. Why had this been so important to her? Was this rebellion?

Only later in life would Dora catch a glimpse of her own prejudice and racism when she had to rely on black women to care for her during her old age. "Better late than never," her daughter would tell her. Watching "All in the Family" would also help her understand the plight of people of color since the program focused on socially-conscious episodes. She would laugh at Archie, but she would identify with Louise and Edith. Dora would learn about race from the sitcoms and sex from the soap operas.

The nineteen seventies extended the culture wars in America. US troops invaded Cambodia, and the antiwar movement grew, resulting in student revolts turning violent when four Kent State students were killed by the National Guard. Beatings and arrests spread across the country. It seemed that the country was in flames, and the rest of the world was boiling. Even the Beatles broke up their band, and the drug-related deaths of Janis Joplin and Jimi Hendrix told the citizens of the world that excess was dangerous.

Was anyone listening? The youth of America who boasted "Don't trust anyone over thirty" were not. Anti-war demonstrators trying to disrupt government and college administration offices were arrested but later released from prison. No one seemed to be safe, either on the right or the left of the political spectrum. George Wallace, governor of Alabama, was shot; the Watergate scandal revealed the corruption of the political structure, and terrorists invaded the Olympics in Munich, Germany

This cultural melt down came close to home as Dora's grandsons experimented with alcohol and drugs and suffered the consequences.

Bill and Dora had always been advocates for washing your dirty laundry at home, not in public, as he had shielded members of his own family and himself from any hint of scandal. Dora did not understand the problem of drugs, but she had an intimate knowledge of alcohol abuse. She remained quiet when she heard about these troubles in the family since, she, too, did not want to risk saying too much. These were not people who believed in full disclosure or talking about one's troubles to strangers.

It was difficult enough for them to share shameful behavior with their relatives. This was the way of "Americans" but not Italian Americans: family business was "handled" in and by the family.

Fear

A shroud of gray envelops,
holding on tightly, breathing slows.
Only the heart beats faster,
dreaded thoughts fill the mind.

Oh for the sun to break through,
release fear, free breath
calm the beating heart.
A golden cloak celebrates release.

gm hanson

Chapter 13
The Beginning of the End

W ith the end of the Vietnam War on April 30, 1975, the lifting of the oil embargo by the OPEC nations, the expansion of the nuclear states, and the continued conflicts in the Middle East, the United States was reeling from problems at home and abroad. American leaders brought the country into a new kind of colonialism because of their might and power.

There never seemed to be enough money or manpower to solve the myriad of conflicts around the globe. At the local levels, civil rights for people of color and for women brought more cultural unrest as many of the groups previously discriminated against brought their causes to the courts and to the television screens throughout the land. News traveled fast as citizens turned to the nightly television news hosted by Chet and David of the Huntley-Brinkley Report or Walter Cronkite.

At the Lucchesi home-front grandchildren now numbered six since Bill and Sandy had two girls and one boy. Sadly their delightful son Daren developed epilepsy adding to the stress on young Bill who had become very involved with his work in a flocking company producing textiles for commercial and domestic use. His job as plant manager and later as chief investor and CEO kept him busy with work and travel. This left his wife in charge of the household, a burden she struggled to manage and control.

Bill and Dora could only stand by and respond when she requested their assistance and watch as she became more insular and distant. They would not initiate, would not assert themselves into their daughter-in-law and son's home life. Bill and Dora knew that there was trouble in paradise but felt helpless and confused since there was nothing they could do about it. As the tension built with children and grandchildren, Bill's stomach condition worsened with time, as he would use alcohol to quell his anxieties and insomnia.

Strangely enough Sandy was using the same treatment. This self-medication strategy was to no avail and would only make matters physiologically and psychologically worse, but in the great family tradition, all was kept quiet. Young Bill did not want to worry his parents, and they did not want to interfere. Whatever happened in these two households would not seep outside. The important value was keeping families together.

Divorce or separation was something this branch of the Lucchesi family would not tolerate. They had been shocked by their nephew Peter's divorce from his first wife and his subsequent liaisons and marriages. Peter had been the favorite child of the clan for many years since he was very intelligent, aloof and charming when he was with individual relatives. He had brought pride to the family from his academic achievements becoming one of the elite who earned a doctorate, but his messy divorce had bewildered his elders. They knew that he was a moody individual, but they could not believe that he had become a family renegade.

"What is wrong here?" Dina would ask Dora. "What is my son thinking? He has three children to support, and now I hear that he and this other woman will have another child. Oh, my God in heaven, what will we do? We must help those kids because his wife is not stable enough to care for them."

"Help as much as you can, Dina. There is only so much you can do living so far away from them. Invite them to your home for a visit or go down there with Norma and check out the situation. You can't abandon the children or his wife who seems so fragile."

"Oh, I know, I know. What did we do coming to this country, Dora? Everything is in turmoil, and now this crazy culture has infested our homes and families."

"It is hard to believe that we are part of this chaos, but I guess that's what we get by wanting to be Americans. I suppose that if we were still in the mountain village we would not be facing these traumas although I hear that sex, drugs and rock 'n roll has made its way to Europe and beyond. The whole world is going out of control."

Both women sat holding each other, trying to comfort and re-assure, but neither one could hold back the tears or inspire much hope in the other.

Adding to their fears were the inevitable signs of illness in their husbands and other relatives. Dora's brothers developed heart and circulatory disease while her sister battled rheumatoid arthritis. Dina had lost one brother to an early cardiac death, had watched her other brother felled by heart disease in his seventies and cried as her only sister succumbed to cancer at sixty-nine. Then her husband, Primo, who had developed diabetes, succumbed to a brain tumor in 1979. A few months following that death, Dora lost her husband to liver cancer. It seemed that the Grim Reaper was mowing down a generation of strong Italian men and women.

Bill's illness had come on swiftly. One day he was in his garden wearing his usual white shirt and watering or gathering vegetables; and the next day he lost interest in his appearance—didn't shave, wore the same clothes for several days at a time until Dora would snatch them in the night when he was asleep. The once energetic Bill began to tire easily, ate little and retreated into himself.

In early September, Dr. Robinson, who had taken care of the family for years, delivered the death sentence—liver cancer—and a dire prognosis. Still reeling from the death of Primo and Sondra, the sister in California, Dora and Dina were devastated by the news. This was not the way it was supposed to be. They had expected to drift into old age with their husbands by their side helping them to assist and support their children and grandchildren.

The next few months were difficult ones for Dora as she struggled to encourage her husband to eat and take care of himself. She was not prepared for his illness or his death. What would she do? She, who had been so dependent on this man who took care of everything financial, she who could not write a check, let alone follow their investments. She had never lived alone since she went from her parents' home to her husband's. Fear and anxiety began to build, taking its toll on her broken heart.

As Bill descended into his illness and became gaunt and pale gray, he shut himself down--away from everyone. His daughter, Gloria, came with her family to spend Thanksgiving with her parents. During the Thanksgiving meal, Bill sat on the couch and stared with those deep blue eyes out the picture window to his beloved lawn and garden. Did he see it or was it a blur? If he did gather the images, he never made a sound, silence his only companion.

The following day, Bill lay in bed, never to sit on the couch again. Fevers, pain and diarrhea accompanied his every move. Gloria decided to stay with Dora and help her during these last few days since she feared for her mother's health. Together they would change, wash and dress him--sheets, diapers, towels were forever being laundered and recycled. Crying out during the night, he would awaken the women who would rush to his side to comfort and console him and each other. His physician, Dr. Robinson, prescribed pain pills and antibiotics, but the cancer cared little for these meager treatments and continued its assault.

"What in the world are we doing?" Gloria asked her mother and brother. "Why are we giving him antibiotics? Prolonging his agony?"

"Let's call the doctor and ask him." responded Bill.

"No, no, we must keep him alive. He will get better soon. He's a strong man and will come out of this," pleaded Dora, the hopeful denier.

No amount of cajoling would dampen Dora's delusion, so Bill and Gloria took control and called the doctor who agreed that this course was futile as was any attempt to challenge Dora's hope.

After a few nights without sleep, Dora and Gloria called for a nurse to take the night shift. Gloria watched as the male nurse picked Bill up under his armpits, sliding him over the side of the bed and onto the bedpan. She observed the nurse as he turned and moved her father so that she could do the same during the day. Bill had always told her to be a nurse. Finally she listened, having a short matriculation and internship in critical care.

The next day as she pulled Bill up from the bed and sat him on the commode, she noticed that Bill's eyes had opened and looked plaintively at her. "Please, please, let me go," she thought she heard him say. Perhaps she was reading his mind. After bathing and dressing him she pulled the clean sheet over his emaciated body, sat by his side and felt the life drain slowly from his feet, his legs, thighs, abdomen, chest and face.

"It's okay, Dad, you can go now. Go to sleep. You can go."

WATCHING DAD GO

Touching the cold bluish ankle
a shiver ran down my spine
watching the life drain from the toes
creeping towards those faded blue eyes
feeling what was left of my father
drifting away, and away and away
fighting back the tears

The horror

The fear

I reached out to pull him back . . . but

he was gone.

gm hanson

Chapter 14
A Widow's Lament

*D*ora, the widow, carried on alone in the home on the hill she and Bill had bought with cash twenty-four years ago. As she roamed the rooms she had once cleaned so fastidiously, she would stop in one chamber where the she would be flooded with memories before moving onto the next. Her daughter had left to return to Cleveland after helping her mother remove the medical equipment they had accumulated to care for Bill along with his clothing and belongings. Gloria feared that these tasks would overwhelm her mother and tip her into depression since she had never learned to drive an automobile, take care of finances, live alone or learn independence.

Dora was a true country girl again, actually feeling as if she were back in her mountain village except that she had running water, a refrigerator, stove and a washing machine. She now slept alone, the most difficult task of her day, in a darkness of the countryside where there were no streetlights, no city lights to lighten the bedroom and render it less frightening. No parents, siblings, husband or children were there to comfort her.

Loneliness hit her one night, and it came in the form of dizziness and flashing lights in her head. She panicked and called her son who rushed over and drove her to the emergency room at Day Kimball Hospital in Putnam. A stroke, albeit mild, was the diagnosis. Feeling weak and unable to speak clearly, she hoped she would be sent home to live with her son and his family, but the doctor discharged her to a rehabilitation facility where she could receive some form of physical therapy, round the clock care and rest. Relatives would come and visit occasionally, but she became too emotional and teary when they left and did not take her with them.

She was now forced to deal with people she did not know or want to be around. She wanted to go home, but of course, that could not happen quickly she was told, but she did not understand why. She would sing the words to the Italian song, "Mamma" where a loving son serenades his mother and promises that she will never be alone. Alas, she knew in her heart of hearts that despite her son's love, she would be alone. She had learned a valuable lesson about patience during these years living in America, one that would help her cope with the waiting—waiting for the day when she could return to her house on the hill.

"Glor, Mom is almost ready to be sent home, but I don't think she can make it there alone. What should we do? She can't come here because we can't give her the care she needs," Bill moaned.

"Well, I'll speak to Richard about having her come here to recuperate. I'm certain that he would want that. He loves Mom and has often told me that we should come up and take her back to Cleveland with us. It is going to be difficult to persuade her, but we will tell her that she can stay here until she is ready to return to her home."

"Can you handle that? You're working and going to school, and this is an added burden."

"I will have someone here to take care of her when I am at work so don't worry about that since we have nurses' aides to provide services for a price."

"She won't have to worry about money because Dad left enough to care for her. The important thing is that she is with her family. She's never been without someone."

"Yes, she was the child bride and in many ways she still is. She's too young to remain in that state so we will have to parent her until she can stand on her own with a little support from us. We can do it, Bill."

"Yes, you and I will keep her safe, big sista. Love ya."

"I love you, too. Tell Mom that she will be visiting here until she gets stronger, that Richard insists, and that we will drive to Connecticut and make a leisurely trip back to Cleveland. That should give her a little hope to work harder and get better."

A few months later Dora was well enough to travel with her daughter and Richard. She expressed mixed feelings about going away from home and her relatives, but as always, she complied with those who were in charge, those who knew better.

She settled into her room on the second floor of Gloria and Richard's Tudor house and accommodated to her new surroundings. Her granddaughter, Daria, was in the bedroom across the hall and shared the bathroom with her. The grandsons, Paul and Ben, lived in bedrooms on the third floor, and the dog and cat roamed the rooms looking for a quiet spot.

Gloria and Richard had tried to make her feel at home with new coverlets for the Victorian bed, draperies for the windows and baseboard electric heaters making this cold home more inviting. The children were so happy to have her since they knew she would cook them some of their favorite food and be there to spoil them.

In the mornings, Dora would sit with Gloria and Richard and have breakfast. He would try to cheer her up with the same question every day.

"Dora, where do you think Bill is this morning? Paradise? Hell? Purgatory?"

Dora would laugh and play along as he continued the narrative with his own opinion.

"I think he is in Purgatory waiting for you to call him up into heaven."

Dora would roll her eyes and wonder whether her husband might not have even made it to Purgatory.

Once everyone had gone to work or school, mother and daughter chatted until Gloria left for class. Dora would begin to talk about her life. She appeared to need this outlet, as she had never shared her thoughts and feelings to anyone, especially not her daughter. Since Gloria was in graduate school for clinical social work and was practicing the art of listening, she was happy to act as a sounding board; but she was not prepared to hear what her mother revealed.

"You know, your father had a drinking problem for many years. He could not sleep and would use whiskey to help him, but he would get up to go to the bathroom and return with a glass of some beverage concoction he had prepared. Between the alcohol, the Valium for his nervousness and his stomach problem, he would spend time vomiting during the night. I used to get up with him, but because he would not consider lowering his alcohol intake, I decided to leave him alone and go back to sleep. There was many a night when I would have to clean up after him."

"My God, Mom, I had no idea. Did you tell anyone?"

"The only person I confided in was your aunt, Dina, who was suffering with the problem drinking of her husband. We would commiserate, but we never told anyone else."

"I do remember seeing Dad drunk on only one occasion. When Bill and Sandy were married, he became so inebriated that he fell out of bed and woke Richard and me. We rushed to him, picked him up and put him back into bed. Richard, feeling his strong pulse, concluded that he had drunk too much, because his heartbeat was so strong and regular. You appeared to be rather casual about the incident so we went back to bed but did not sleep well, waiting for the other shoe to drop. The next morning he arose to get ready for church and acted as if nothing happened. We three looked so tired with reddened eyes and weary looks, but Dad looked great, tanned and trim."

"Oh yes, I remember that. I was so angry with him I could hardly look at him during the reception. He embarrassed me in front of Richard and his parents whom I thought had heard his midnight thump."

"He maintained that he had eaten something that made him sick. I wonder if he remembered what happened the night before or if he didn't want to talk about it."

"Food was always his excuse."

"How long was this going on?"

"Your father always drank, but in the past ten years when he tried to treat his insomnia, he became worse. When he was younger he would also see other women."

"What?"

"I am saying that family members and I believe he was seeing someone. I had no way to check this, but all the signs of infidelity were there. Your uncles and aunts talked to him about it, but I think it was only when his health seriously deteriorated that he stopped."

"It is so hard for me to hear all of this. I always thought he was a flirt around women, but I never suspected this. Does Bill know any of this?"

"No, I don't think he would believe it, and I always thought that he would get angry and not come around to see me or think I was a crazy old lady."

More stories, more secrets, more family history spilled out during these morning breakfasts. Dora was finally addressing the anger and sadness she had been burying in her heart for so many years. As a widow she was finally being heard.

Secrets

Don't tell anyone—ever.
lie if you must—seal lips.
Privacy is a secure shell
keeping us from harm.

Our fragile, soft underbellies
are to be protected at all costs.
Sharp teeth, saw jaws search
far into our deepest thoughts.

Beware the savage, secret scavenger.

Oh no, I cannot comply.
I heed the Russian sage.
"Families are only as sick
as the secrets they keep."

Sea plankton float in transparency,
open to sun and predators alike.
Somehow these vulnerable ones
thrive in their open freedom.

Beware the sordid selfishness of secrets.

gm hanson

Ben, Daria, Paul

Bill, Dora and grandchildren

Darcy, Sandy, Bill, Tara, Daren

Dora at the Trevi Fountains - Rome, 1984

Chapter 15
Independence at a Price

*T*he nineteen-eighties were a fractious time as President Jimmy Carter left office with inflation roaring and 7.1 per cent of the population out of work. American nuns were being killed, hostages were taken in Iran, world leaders like Anwar el-Sadat of Egypt and Indira Gandhi of India were assassinated, John Lennon of the Beatles was killed, and the Pope was wounded by a gunman. All of these events challenged the peace-loving President. By the time he left the White House to Ronald Reagan, he had become a pariah to the American people who saw him as weak and incompetent.

1983 saw an escalation of violence against Americans as 237 Marines died in a terrorist explosive attack in Beirut, Lebanon, while on the home front the development of "crack cocaine" in the Bahamas would disable and kill many more citizens than our formal enemies. Unemployment reached 9.6% and as inflationary pressures were retreating in the United States, terrorists increased their attacks by hijacking the Italian cruise ship, *Achille Lauro*, capturing a TWA plane, taking hostages, and seizing an Egyptian Boeing 737 airliner.

In mid decade, major chemical leaks in India, nuclear accidents at Chernobyl and explosions of the space shuttle at its launching rattled the world community. Later, in 1988 terrorists killed nine tourists on a cruise ship and a Pan-Am 747 exploded from a terrorist bomb, crashing in Lockerbie, Scotland. The US began to retaliate in 1989 shooting down two Libyan fighters in the Mediterranean, while tens of thousands of Chinese students cried out for more democracy and were gunned down in Tiananmen Square. New enemies rose up against the United States and western culture bringing more chaos and anxiety to the American people.

Positive news for the democracies of the world included the tearing down of the Berlin Wall and the fall of many Communist-led countries. President Ronald Reagan, appearing both tough and a fighter for capitalism and less government interference in the lives of ordinary Americans and the business community, had presided over these many events for two terms, His vice president, George Bush, a patrician and Texas oilman, succeeded him, winning the election with a landslide vote. Dora thought the new President was handsome and empathized with the portly Barbara.

Dora's life became more complex. Her return from Cleveland and the move from her home on the hill in Brooklyn to a condominium for retirees in Danielson, enabled her to take public transportation for seniors to shop and get out among people; however, old habits don't change easily.

She resisted taking the bus, as she wanted her son or daughter-in-law to take her grocery shopping, and she refused to attend the senior center for bingo within her condominium complex. She awaited family company and had no interest in making new friends. Unfortunately, her son and his family, her nephews and nieces and her out-of-town daughter were raising their own families where time was a commodity in short supply.

In November, Dora decided to pack up and re-visit

her daughter in Cleveland. She was probably the only American citizen to go to Cleveland for a few winter months. She was not a snowbird in the popular parlance, being more like a bird chasing the snow.

Once there she would once again enter into the family life by cooking and keeping herself busy with grandchildren and television, learning a great deal from the soap operas such as "Days of Our Lives," especially when it came to love and romance, addiction and infidelity. She would love to hear the "Three Tenors" sing opera or "O Sole Mio," an ode to the sun of which there wasn't much during Cleveland winters. The Christmas mass from Rome would keep her awake until after midnight when the family could not transport her to the cathedral for the service due to snow, sleet or hazardous road conditions. She was content being in the bosom of her family and did not care about lake snow, grey days or cold winds from Lake Erie.

Unfortunately, her heart and circulatory system continued to be troublesome. A pacemaker, blood pressure pills and heart medication stabilized her so that when her daughter asked her if she would like to travel back to Italy in September, she happily said, "Yes, yes."

Landing in Rome, Dora and Gloria settled into the facilities at a local convent for foreign tourists. Gloria would then take her awed mother to visit the Vatican, the Coliseum or museums when energy allowed. One of her favorite spots was the Trevi Fountain where she could rest and admire the sculpture and watch the calming waters.

The duo then boarded a train to Florence where they would once again see the sights since Dora had never had the opportunity to appreciate her homeland treasures. She had left when she was young and while her country was on the brink of war, and when she traveled with her own family, she had became a village housewife and did not visit the famous cities of Italy as a tourist.

Gloria rented a small Italian Fiat, and mother and daughter made their way to Bagni di Lucca—Riolo, traveling those winding dirt roads that once had borne the boots of peasants and soldiers, and now bore the marks of rubber tires kicking up the dust of history. Arriving in the village where she was born and had not visited in more than forty years, Dora was overcome with emotion. She visited her parents' home that had been left to the inadequate care of a local resident, and she cried and grieved over the faded photos on the walls and in the trunk lying in the bedroom.

Seeing the fireplace, the scattered furniture, the bed where her mother had died drowned her in sorrow. The arrival of one her old friends on the doorstep lifted her from her doldrums. Pellagrina, a childhood friend, who visited Riolo every summer, would take her to the town center where a small group of villagers, early childhood companions who had stayed behind in the old country, gathered to greet her. Those still living in Riolo looked the way the elders of the village had looked sixty-five years ago—kerchiefed and darkly clothed in tribute to their dead spouses.

There had been a few changes in Riolo—some houses had electricity, but hardly any had running water or indoor plumbing. Going there was like stepping back in time. Visiting the cemetery where the dead were buried on top of each other as time passed and as land became scarce for the churches, Dora gazed at the pictures of her parents on the sanctuary wall and wished she could have been there for them during their illnesses instead of being thousands of miles away. Her father had owned many acres of land in those mountains; and at this time, they lay fallow and untended, practically worthless. Would anyone find this beautiful place and resurrect it?

Years later, Dora was to discover that wealthy Europeans and some Americans would indeed buy these old properties for second homes, while Italians looking to escape the cities would begin to live and resuscitate these mountain enclaves. The trip was a huge success for Dora who would regale her relatives in Connecticut about what and whom she had seen. Turning the pages of the photo album and reminiscing became her favorite pastime when she returned home to Danielson.

She had caught the travel bug and expressed a desire to travel to see relatives in St. Louis and Chicago. Gloria would oblige her. She also developed a long lost interest in her appearance, loved to go shopping and buy new clothes for herself, and treat herself to her favorite hairdresser who had persuaded her to let her dyed hair turn a beautiful snowy white. She visited Florida with Gloria and Richard and rode around in a wheel chair at Epcot Center and the Busch Gardens after complaining that she did not want to be seen "in one of those things."

Once Dora became accustomed to the ease and comfort she would ask if the chair had been stored in the trunk when she went to see her heartthrob, Perry Como or out to the mall to shop and have lunch. She had become so excited about her new life that she decided to vote for Geraldine Ferraro for Vice President when she returned home in the summer; however, she had never registered. Gloria obliged her on one of her visits to Connecticut, and now she was a registered voter, ready to vote for an Italian-American woman. The only remaining obstacle was getting her to the polls on Election Day, but she suffered another disappointment since no one appeared at her door.

A few weeks later, Dora was hospitalized again by a cerebral accident. More of her faculties were compromised, and the family decided that she could not live alone. Once again, they packed up her belongings and moved her to Cleveland. This was to be a temporary move for she insisted that she wanted to spend her remaining days in the Catholic nursing home in Connecticut where family could visit. At the moment, however, there were no openings forcing her to wait in Cleveland. She was good at waiting.

Her life in Cleveland was pleasant enough. She would ride the escalator to her bedroom and family room where she spent many hours watching television or talking to Katie, the standard poodle, her constant companion. An African-American aide would care for her while Gloria worked. Ethel and Dora would become very close, as Ethel would bathe her, do her hair and assist her as her health deteriorated; and Dora would tell her how to cook Italian food.

In summer they would go for short walks in the yard, the dog following behind as the two women slowly meandered. Dora had come a long way from the prejudicial younger woman living in an all white community. She enjoyed "All in the Family" and loved to watch as Edith and Louise tried to cope with their pigheaded husbands. She could certainly identify with their feelings. The show taught her that people with a different skin color had the same problems as she did— the same sorrows and joys. To the amazement of her family, she would laugh and nod her head at the commentary and comedic routine of the political satirist, Mark Russell, who would use old standard tunes to attach new, humorous lyrics to parody political events of the day. As her life had expanded so had her view of the world.

One day in late summer the call from Matulitis, the Catholic nursing home, arrived. Dora was ready to go home, a place she had romanticized and filled with fantasies of reunions with relatives and grandchildren. Richard and Gloria tried to dissuade her, grandchildren called with their entreaties, and her son warned her of loneliness and isolation. This was all to no avail.

Gloria and Richard packed her things and drove her to Connecticut and settled her into her stark hospital-like room. Dora would have a roommate, and a shared bathroom since there were no private rooms available. She looked around and tried not to cry as Gloria unpacked her clothing into the shared closet and bureau. The staff welcomed her and re-assured her that she would like it there, would enjoy the food, the activities and the daily masses, and that everything would be taken care of by the nurses and aides.

Dora and Gloria looked out the second-floor window onto the lovely grounds of the facilities, paths to walk on, flowers to smell and trees for nesting birds. She could enjoy all of these pleasures, but in her heart she was apprehensive as she said good-bye to her daughter who promised she would visit again soon.

The reality of the nursing home would become painfully aware to Dora within the next few days. Her roommate was not too friendly nor gracious, but was envious of Dora's pretty clothes and loving family. Sharing a bathroom with this woman and the men who occupied the suite on the other side left Dora with a sinking feeling. Being a woman who valued cleanliness next to godliness, she moaned when entering the bathroom and finding urine on the toilet and floor. She had spent many years cleaning up after her husband and now must she do the same with strangers?

When Gloria called to inquire about the re-settlement process a week later, Dora began to cry, "I want to come home. I hate this place! I made a mistake."

Having been warned by her brother of Dora's un-happiness and constant barrage of complaints, Gloria was prepared.

"Of course you can come home, Mom. Let's see how you feel in a week since you haven't had time to become adjusted."

"I will never adjust to this place, my roommate, the food, the room. Never, never, never. I would rather die than stay here."

"Well, Richard and I will let you know when we can drive to Connecticut to bring you home. Remember, Mom, this is a two-day trip, and we are still working. I will call to see if I can arrange care for you and get things in order so be patient."

"I will try, but my capacity for patience is wearing thin."

Within the month, Dora was happily ensconced in her own bedroom, sleeping in her own bed and using her own bathroom. Nothing had been changed. The flowered bed covers and soft carpet were there to greet and comfort her as was her aging companion, Katie, who wagged her tail and barked with delight when she saw her old friend coming up the stairs.

Within a few years, more transient ischemic epi-sodes blew holes in her brain as the slow march to-wards death brought her once again to a dependent state. She would have trouble speaking, swallowing and walking. Congestive heart failure and pneumonia crippled her body and spirit. Under the blankets, she became a collection of bones and dust held together by sheer willpower. Drawing more and more into herself she was a tiny lady with silver white hair and cellophane skin who could not dress or feed herself.

Gloria had called her brother one evening in June of 1992 and told him that he had better come to Cleveland if he wanted to see his Mom alive.

"I don't know how long she has to live, Bill. She is weak and febrile, has developed congestive heart failure, eats little and stares out into space."

"I will leave this afternoon and drive straight through to Cleveland."

The next morning Dora awoke at 7:30AM and was sitting in her Lazy Girl chair. Gloria had made her some warm oatmeal and was feeding her small teaspoonfuls so that Dora could swallow at least some of the cereal, the rest would dribble down her chin onto her nightgown and robe. Her pretty face was haunted by strokes, her once rotund body shrunken to a shadow of her former self.

"Isn't it time for me to go?" Dora asked, looking up at her daughter with those faded blue eyes.

Shocked and speechless at her mother's question, Gloria answered in a hesitant voice, "Maybe it is, Mom, maybe it is, but now let's get you ready to see Bill and Daren. They should be here within the hour."

She helped her Mother get out of the chair and took her to the bathroom where Dora took care to properly shield herself. Gloria helped her up, held onto her arm as she led her through the guest room towards her own room.

As she rounded the corner of the bathroom Dora collapsed. Gloria could do nothing to break her fall and called for Richard to help her lift her mother who had fallen on her back with one leg on the bathroom tile and one on the bedroom carpet. Gloria was cradling her mother's head in her lap, feeling her mother now as a spirit woman, when Richard knelt down and spoke softly to Dora.

"Dora, I want you to lift this right leg when I say three so I can pick it up and put it near your other leg. Then we can lift you and return you to bed so you can rest."

"One, two, three" . . . and Dora, the compliant, sweet one who had never wanted to disappoint or to need much from others in return for her love, took one deep breath, lifted her leg and fell into paradise.

Dora Lucchesi died on June 12, 1992 at the age of 81 years and 5 days.

Il Sospiro (The breath)

The brain reels from constant attacks,
blowing holes in that convoluted mass.
The energy flow forms a trickle,
eyes seek far away places,
feet shuffle towards the bed,
bones become porously brittle,
swallowing silences the appetite
as wobbly legs buckle.
One long sospiro brings relief.

gm hanson
May, 2009

Afterwords --

Family, friends and editors asked me if I had learned anything about myself in writing this creative nonfiction about my mother. Although I was in the book as a child and adult, I did not see any parallels between my life and hers; and certainly, I viewed myself as being more like my Dad than my Mom. I did not consider her as much of a role model when I was young, wanting to be the opposite of her in my own life, independent, adventurous and seeking my own identity. The questions, however, prompted me to write a Part II in which I would be interviewed by some fictional interviewer and be forced to look at the lives of My Mother, Myself.

Conversations with the author, Gloria Lucchesi Hanson

Tell us how you came to want to write this book at this time in your life.

Well, the idea came to me in that twilight time just before awakening. I had retired from my practice as a clinical social worker and was thinking about what I was going to do with the next ten to fifteen years of my life. Volunteer, grandchild sit, learn bridge again, knit, work part time selling lingerie at Saks? All of this brainstorming was brewing in my head for weeks. I had been writing poetry and prose for years as an avocation and recently researching a family history. I had accumulated information from taped interviews, conversations and family records. This started me thinking about my own life—the warp and woof of it—what influenced me, what did it mean, where was I going? I started wondering what my own mother's life had been like, how she and I were alike—what skin we shared.

What did you discover?

Well, as a child I learned that I was as different from my mom as night is to day. She had been the obedient, compliant daughter of a domineering mother while I, on the other hand, had been disobedient, non-conforming and non-accommodating to any adult figure. She was the baby in her family with 3 brothers and one sister thirteen years older than she. I was the first born in a family of 2. Her childhood experiences were marked by constant comings and goings of her father and siblings. Parents and relatives, on the other hand, enveloped me —always there, always hovering, sometimes suffocating.

What effect did this have on you?

I can only guess, but I think I was uncomfortable with this enmeshed family mass, wanting to escape, eat only what I wanted, stay alone, keep others out of my space. My cousin, Peter, tells me a story of having to knock on the inner sanctum of my bedroom to visit for a short while, all the while wondering whether I was "receiving." This kind of behavior was alien to a family of talkers, eaters and visitors—I call it the village way—thereby turning me into a strange child who could easily be left on the sidelines and better left alone.

If you were this way as a child, you must have been a terror as an adolescent.

By today's standards, I was an angel adolescent—or at least an angel in training. My Dad, having an intimate knowledge of this wild, out-of-control stage, decided to step up his strict parenting forays by limiting my outside activities and checking my every move. In response, I became more defensive, secretive and determined to outwit these parental figures, Mom and Dad, aunts, uncles and older cousins, since living within an extended family meant that everyone knew every one else's business and could step in to give good or bad advice.

My Mom particularly suspected I was up to no good since I reminded her of my dad, known for sneaking around, and herself who ran off at age 16 to marry a stranger whom she had known for an entire two months. She would investigate my whereabouts and report back to my father who would then take action. They were totally confused, since they did not want to corral my involvement in school activities such as Drama or Debating Club, but they did not want me to abuse the freedom these opportunities provided. I became a master of subterfuge, a maven of deception as I did what I had to do, in order to do what I wanted. Just as my mother had the cooperation of her father during her courtship, I had the devotion and complicity of my little brother who would cover for me.

You must have been so happy to leave for college. Did you change your behavior once you escaped?

I attended a Catholic college so there was a built in oversight as colleges in those days assumed the "*in locus parentis*" philosophy, but there were always ways to get around rules. I would get my fun from being free from 9AM to 7PM, curfew time, on Saturdays to explore New York City. My parents never knew where I was or what I was doing. My mother did not experience any sense of personal freedom until she was in her seventies, but then she was limited by the dependency of her previous years and by encroaching poor health.

With all of this deception, were you a sexually active young woman who was out of step with her time?

Oh no, my father used to sing the "avoid pregnancy" song, instilling fear in my heart of terrible things that would ensue from an early pregnancy. In addition, I believed in the Catholic ideal of womanhood. It made sense to me even when boys would call me a "tease" or a goody-goody Catholic girl, but it was difficult to resolve the conflict between my head and my heart. My boyfriend dumped me in my sophomore year at college, and I turned to the liturgy, refined to high art at my college. I loved matins, masses with choral music and incense, and the prayers at midday. Meditating, saying the Stations of the Cross and reading sacred texts helped me get over the break up and even consider the life of a Carmelite nun, one who lived in silence. I finally came to the conclusion that I would not be a good nun—too much submission, and since I could not pursue a career in medicine because of a lack of funding, I decided to become a scientist like my mentor, Dr. Mary Rogick, who taught and did research on plankton. She encouraged and supported me as a laboratory assistant as I pithed frogs for class and collected specimen for her by Long Island Sound. I was convinced that I was destined to be like her—a scholar and a spinster—a form of religious life.

What happened? I thought you retired recently as a psychotherapist.

I attended Brown University graduate school on an assistantship, meaning that I would work for free tuition and a meager stipend. During my first week on campus, I met a fellow student at a French qualifying exam. That did it! I was smitten and gave up my planned destiny of scholastic solitude. We were married when I received my Master's Degree in 1961. I was 25—an old bride at that time. The thinking during the early sixties was that a woman should have children by age 30; after that one might have a Down's Syndrome child so I thought I would teach for one year and then try to become pregnant. Having carried my strong conviction against artificial birth control from my college years, I convinced myself and my husband that the rhythm method could work, and that we would succeed. Indeed, we did succeed—in having 2 boys in nineteen-and-one-half months. As I lay in a hospital bed recovering from delivering my second child during the spring break period at my college, a strange event occurred. My roommate was a tired looking 45-year-old Catholic woman with 9 children, a creature in a fog, barely audible and eager to extend her stay in the hospital. I thought to myself, "God, not the Church, is speaking to me."

Needless to say, I began looking at mortal sin and its consequences versus high-minded virtue and decided to take a detour for self-preservation. Science came to my rescue in the
form of a birth control pill. Now I could teach at a local college with help from my parents who lived about 45 minutes
away. Both retirees, they were all the more willing to work
around my schedule to be near their grandchildren; and since
I had not been indoctrinated in the bonding or the nursing
philosophy, I was willing to let them go, stay with relatives as
I had been raised, receive milk from the bottle, and bond with
their grandparents. Dr. Spock had spoken.

When I play "What If?" I wonder what we would have done
without Dora and Bill. Would Richard have had to quit graduate school because we could not live on his meager stipend
or find affordable and available babysitters? What if I had
remained in graduate school instead of convincing myself to
have children before the age of 30? What if I had decided to
pursue, not delay my career to be a parent? Ah, those forks in
the road! When one is young and wondering whether women
could have it all, I, like my mother, failed to ask why men
should have it all and demand equal time for oneself. My
mother had a desire to go to school to learn English, but she
set her needs aside to build a business and my father's career.
The choices are similar.

In 1966 my husband and I decided to have another child, a
daughter being the gender of choice. We were successful in
producing a blonde, blue-eyed little girl. Being at home with
3 children with only a part time job translating scientific arti-
cles for journals, I decided that pursuing my doctorate in science would be so demanding on my young family that I chose
instead to switch fields after spending a few years volunteer-
ing. I began taking courses in psychology and sociology.
Later I received my social work degree in Cleveland, but my
career was never number one on my list since I thought that
taking care of the little souls I had brought to this earth out-

ranked my own needs.

Again it was quite evident that I was my mother's daughter at heart. While I openly expressed my frustration and sense of societal injustice to anyone who would listen, I did not fully embrace the total message of the feminist movement. I added my voice, but women who wanted more than parity drowned it out. I was by then the compromiser, convinced that something is better than nothing—my mother, myself. The number of years in school did not matter. Both illiterate mother and educated daughter came to the same conclusion.

How do you see your later years as being like your mother?

It seems that I have managed to escape the dependency curse visited upon my mother in her later years since my health is good as is my marriage to a loyal husband. My children have remained in touch and solicitous, especially my daughter, who despite early mother-daughter conflicts has drawn closer to me since she became a mother. The close family ties to the extended family were never strong after I left home at eighteen, but my mother had only those linkages as a lifeline since socializing or developing female friends outside the family were next to impossible or were not encouraged. I have developed strong ties to women friends wherever I have lived and retain those even now. They are my lifelines. Friends of varying degrees, bosom buddies to share my woes and worries, social friends to enjoy activities together, walking friends, gym friends and movie friends. A few of my cousins have re-entered my life in the past few years and have been a way to re-connect to my roots. My bond with my husband combines friendship, companionship, partnering in most things—an intimacy I don't believe my mom ever experienced, being a young woman separated from parents, country, customs and becoming involved in the all-consuming job of making a living.

And how alike are you?

We both lived with violence, death, despair, terror in the air
we breathed since the twentieth century specialized in wars,
genocide and violence against the human spirit. Unfortunately, for me, this continues into this century. We knew
about war but did not experience it on a personal level. Dora
railed against President Lyndon Johnson because she thought
he was going to take her son while I marched and petitioned
against the Viet Nam war because I thought it was an unjust
war, one that could possibly linger long enough to involve my
sons.

I am a loyal caretaker and involved grandmother as was she;
but as she was silent with her children about child rearing and
marriage, I share my thoughts and feelings, albeit, a tad too
much, struggling with boundaries—that healthy distance with
my children.

I, too, love my wonderful son-in-law as my dear mother did
my husband. My daughters-in-law are cherished for their devotion to their families and their show of love and affection
for their in-laws. In many ways Dora was a template for the
unfolding of my life. My grandchildren have brought joy and
vigor to my life just as they did my mother, and I yearn to
spend time with them and share my enthusiasms for the world
around us. I, unlike my mother, do not reward them with
M&M's.

I have stood by my man during his battle with chronic lym-
phocytic leukemia, chemotherapy and respiratory nightmares.
I battle his disease along with him, refusing to let him go
without a fight. Both mom and I were loyal handmaidens,
ready to go the extra mile for those we love, fighting despair
and remaining present.

When all is said and done, I am my mother's daughter in loving solitude, family, a braided routine and life's little pleasures. Some things hold and stay in place.

Gloria Hanson is a retired clinical social worker who has written as an avocation for much of her life. She has recently placed writing at the very top of her 'retirement bliss' list. Her words comprise poems, essays, book reviews, non-fiction, and more recently—fiction.

She has long puzzled over the life and experiences of her immigrant parents—especially her mother, who left Italy at such a young age, with little or no knowledge of the English language. Zora not only survived—she even thrived! How did she learn or even know what she knew? It is indeed a puzzlement.

Made in the USA
Charleston, SC
28 February 2010